Praise for *Hacking Sales*

"Companies that embrace technology and data in their sales process will build the world class sales organizations that win. *Hacking Sales* creates an actionable, cutting-edge sales process that can scale with your sales org and the ever-changing world of technology."

—**Mark Roberge**, Chief Revenue Officer, HubSpot

"Max's sorted through the maelstrom of sales and marketing apps out there to cut through the clutter and show us some creative and practical ways to automate sales drudgery. Well done, sir!"

—**Aaron Ross**, Built Outbound Sales at Salesforce; Cofounder, Predictable Revenue and Carb.io

"*Hacking Sales* succinctly shows sellers how to use new technology and sales tactics to up their game."

—**Elay Cohen**, Former SVP of Sales Productivity, Salesforce; Cofounder and CEO, SalesHood

"Max has become a dominant force in the next wave of sales: the use of technology, training, and best practices to turn sales into a true science. Sales can truly now be hacked much in the way we learned in the last generation to hack marketing into a quantitative growth engine. *Hacking Sales* has uniquely captured these changes, bringing together sales thought leadership and leading next-generation technologies together to quantify and scale sales dramatically faster than ever before. Kudos, and thank you, to Max."

—**Jason Lemkin**, Cofounder and ex-CEO, Echosign; Founder, SaaStr; Managing Director, Storm Ventures

"Traditional sales methods have not kept pace with how customers want to buy today. Sales technology is finally catching up to the market and Max has created the ultimate playbook on how to sell in this era of Sales Acceleration."

—**Gary Swart**, Former CEO, Upwork; Partner, Polaris Partners

"Max is at the forefront of this new age of selling and has done a fantastic job in this book outlining the process of building and evolving a sales approach and process with tools, tips, and techniques along the way. I recommend it to any sales rep or sales leader who is looking to play catch up or stay ahead of this ever-evolving profession we call Sales."

—**John Barrows**, Leading Sales Trainer for Salesforce, LinkedIn, Zendesk, Marketo, Box, and many of the world's top technology sales organizations

"Max has packed this book full of actionable advice that will allow any sales professional to cut through the clutter and immediately improve results, by using proven techniques and tools. If you are an individual contributor or early stage founder looking to accelerate growth, reading this book will be the highest ROI you will get from your time today."

—**Matt Cameron**, Former Global Head of Corporate Sales, Yammer; VP of Sales, Kahuna

"Sales is undergoing such a major transformation; some would say so much that the profession may be at risk. Max has responded by starting a movement where sales professionals can share and learn from each other regularly through thought leadership, events, community, and networking. This book is a critical must-have component to anyone who wants to stay ahead of this transformation."

—**Emmanuelle Skala**, VP of Sales, Influitive

"Finally! A single, consolidated playbook to help start-ups define their prospecting strategy and sales philosophy. Max breaks down the areas to consider and the tools to evaluate in helping you maximize your resources. A great read for any VP Sales who's building their team out."

—**Bill Binch**, VP of World Wide Sales, Marketo

"As sales becomes more scientific, sales teams need to stay up to date on all the new technologies and processes. Max Altschuler knows them all!"

—**Armando Mann**, VP of Sales, RelateIQ

"Max is one of the original hackers, and like all hackers he's full of tips and tricks for you to follow and swallow to master the game of sales. It doesn't matter how much experience you have selling; you will most certainly gain some new knowledge by reading this book. It is chock full of unique ideas and approaches for you to use. This is a must-read for anyone just getting into sales.

—**Doug Landis**, VP of Sales Productivity, Box

"Max Altschuler and the Sales Hacker team are always on point. They remain at the forefront of knowing what's hip, what's now, and what's driving revenue for today's sales organizations. The tools and technologies explored in this book will bring you to the front of the line—on your sales team, in your industry, and at your bank."

—**Ralph Barsi, Sr.**, Director of Sales Development at ServiceNow

"Over the last few years, the sales development field has strongly emerged as the biggest innovation to happen to the sales process. There are not many who are more educated on this than Max Altschuler. Max shares his insights here as one of the only real references you'll need to understand this emerging space. After a quick read, you'll be able to boost revenue for your business and double down on your knowledge of modern day selling."

—**Kyle Porter**, Cofounder and CEO, SalesLoft

"Max has spent the last five years not only working in the trenches of B2B sales teams; he's also networked and collaborated with the most talented practitioners as part of his growing Sales Hacker movement. In this book, he has been gracious enough to share truly actionable strategies that just don't get written about in traditional cookie cutter sales books. For both sales leaders and salespeople, this is a must-read."

—**Tawheed Kader**, Founder and CEO, ToutApp

"I've been lucky to have a first-row seat watching Max create a new school of sales over the past few years. His real-world experience, constant optimization, and questioning of traditional sales norms have created the best practices in this book that are essential for any sales team."

—**Jaspar Weir**, Cofounder and President, TaskUs

"*Hacking Sales* is the definitive guide to building a powerful sales machine that leverages the wide range of technology and data available today. Max has delivered a gift to sales reps and managers everywhere."

—**Ryan Buckley**, Cofounder and Head of Sales, Scripted

HACKING SALES

The Ultimate Playbook and Tool Guide to Building a High-Velocity Sales Machine

MAX ALTSCHULER

WILEY

Published by John Wiley & Sons, Inc., Hoboken, New Jersey.
Published simultaneously in Canada.

For general information about our other products and services, please contact our Customer Care Department within the United States at (800) 762-2974, outside the United States at (317) 572-3993 or fax (317) 572-4002.

Wiley publishes in a variety of print and electronic formats and by print-on-demand. Some material included with standard print versions of this book may not be included in e-books or in print-on-demand. If this book refers to media such as a CD or DVD that is not included in the version you purchased, you may download this material at http://booksupport.wiley.com. For more information about Wiley products, visit www.wiley.com.

ISBN 978-1-119-28164-1 (cloth);
ISBN 978-1-119-28165-8 (ePDF);
ISBN 978-1-119-28167-2 (ePub)

Printed in the United States of America

10   9   8   7   6   5   4   3   2   1

CONTENTS

AUTHOR'S NOTE

The companies mentioned in this book are not in any way affiliated with Sales Hacker, Inc. We take no fees or compensation from any of the companies mentioned in this book. The companies listed are in no particular rank or order. I provide information and my opinion, but it's up to the reader to decide which companies to do business with and what process to follow.

Visit www.SalesHacker.com for more information and bonus material.

INTRODUCTION

WHY SALES, WHY NOW?

The world of sales is blowing up. It's a $500 billion industry that employs over 15 million people in the United States alone. Salesforce, a company that focuses predominantly on sales technology, may soon be doing $10 billion in annual recurring revenue (ARR). For reference, that comes close to what the National Football League made in revenue in 2015.

Sales itself is undergoing a transformation. One could call it the sales acceleration or sales automation era. There is more financial investment in sales, and more talented people are choosing careers in sales than ever before. The Ivy Leaguers who once would have jumped straight into finance jobs at Goldman Sachs are getting into the sales game instead. Big venture capital firms are funding sales automation and acceleration start-ups. There are more cash-rich companies that have capital to spend on natural acquisitions than ever before. It's a good time to be in sales.

Business executives are realizing that a good sales team will make or break their business. In a Stanford computer science lecture on distribution, Peter Thiel, one of Silicon Valley's most outspoken angel investors, said:

> The first thing to do is to dispel the belief that the best product always wins. There is a rich history of instances where the best product did not, in fact, win. Nikola Tesla invented the alternating current electrical supply system. It was, for a variety of reasons, technologically better than the direct current system that Thomas Edison developed. Tesla was the better scientist. But Edison was the better businessman, and he went on to start GE. Interestingly, Tesla later

developed the idea of radio transmission. But Marconi took it from him and then won the Nobel Prize. Inspiration isn't all that counts. The best product may not win.

Thiel, who has been a part of some of the most successful technology companies of the past two decades (PayPal, Facebook, Yelp, Palantir, and many more), is worth over $2 billion, and he comes from a product background.

Sales is in everything you do.

Yet, with all of these facts, only a handful of colleges offer degrees in sales, and most Master of Business Administration (MBA) programs don't offer a single class in sales. That is why I'm writing this book.

As the marketplace rapidly changes, there are so many new things to take advantage of as a modern-day salesperson. Consider reading this book as your enrollment in a class—the beginning of your degree in modern sales. I call it Sales Hacking.

Who This Book Is For

This book was written for anyone who is in a sales role. To be more specific, this book is for:

- The individual sales reps who want to get ahead of their peers and be at the top of their organization
- One of your company's first few sales hires who has to sell and create a process as he or she goes along
- The early stage company with a cofounding team that is looking to build a sales process that they can bring in experienced salespeople to run
- Anyone building a sales process in which he or she is selling to an entity, such as a business, a government, or another type of organization. This is called business-to-business, or B2B, sales.

WHERE THIS BOOK FITS IN

- Your company has a sales process, but it was built in the Prohibition Era.

- You have a sales process, and it is working out well, but you're working too hard.

- You have a product market fit and some paying customers, but you need to know what to do next.

WHAT THIS BOOK IS NOT

- *Start-up Sales 101. Hacking Sales* won't help you get a product market fit, validate ideas, give you a lean start-up methodology, and so on. If you want to learn more about start-up sales, read Steli Efti's short book, *The Ultimate Startup Guide to Outbound Sales*, which I recommend for learning more about these topics.

- *The answer to all of your problems.* You're still going to have to figure out what works for your individual business. Every business is different. This book is a guide that can help you figure those things out on your own.

- *A guide on how to hire, train, and manage teams. Hacking Sales* is for sellers, hunters, and deal-closers.

Having a sales process for your business is extremely important. Without it, your business will be disorganized and disjointed. If you're not tracking and measuring with a standardized approach, then how will you get better? The best assets of sales teams and salespeople are great organizational and analytical skills. Companies that figure this out early and build a strong and streamlined engine will surpass their competitors. Sales reps who figure this out will outsell their peers.

This book was written to help you build a strong foundation for your business. Specifically, this book will help you to do the following:

- Build a pipeline in a repeatable and scalable manner that can be refined and enhanced over time

- Close deals faster and nurture leads properly

- Take advantage of all of the new technologies that make selling more efficient

This book can be used at any stage of a B2B business. Some companies will use this book later on to strengthen an existing business. Some will use it early and build from scratch. Consider this book as your playbook.

A lot of books claim to have all of the answers, which is, of course, impossible. In the end, all companies are made differently. Different variables such as industry, country, deal size, deal cycle, and target buyers affect outcomes greatly.

While I don't promise to serve you the answers on a silver platter, I will put you on the path to find them for yourself. I'll talk about problems and solutions as generally as possible; just understand that parts of the process vary greatly for different companies. The timing of sending out e-mails and other communications that I explain later in this book may be drastically different from what yours should be, for many reasons. There are so many variables at play. Take this book as a guide, but don't blindly follow it. Always test and optimize suggestions to find what's right for you.

Most of the book will focus on outbound sales. However, much of the advice will work for inbound sales as well; for example, segmenting, messaging, and lead research are relevant to both.

Regardless of how many inbound leads you have, you should be doing some level of outbound selling. Always be on the hunt. If your inbound leads are good, you'll have cash to pay the base salary for an outbound seller. If people come to you and want your services, others who haven't found you may show the same interest. Go upstream, aim high, and go get them!

Visit www.SalesHacker.com/library for more resources and bonus material on each section in this book.

CHAPTER 1

Developing Your Sales Stack

The Sales Stack is the technology you use throughout the sales process to engage potential buyers and to facilitate them at each stage of your pipeline. This should be a repeatable and scalable system that runs from the top of the pipeline down to the hand-off after you have signed a contract.

WHERE DO I START?

To get started, ask yourself two things: "What stages of the pipeline matter most to me?" and "What are the milestones that I want to hit along the way?" Don't list too many stages, as they can confuse you as you scale your business.

Your pipeline might look something like Figure 1.1:

CONTACTED > QUALIFIED > DEMO > PROPOSAL > CLOSED

Figure 1.1 Pipeline

I recommend that each stage has its own checklist. For example, in the "Closed" stage, make sure you ask for referrals. In the "Proposal" stage, you may want to use a product to track in order to see what page of the proposal the customer is looking at, and follow up on it.

The main things that matter when you are managing a pipeline are the following:

- Total number of deals in the pipeline

- Average deal size
- Percent of deals that move from stage to stage until they are closed
- Average time a deal stays in the pipeline

You'll want to find baseline numbers to measure each stage of the sales process. Be extremely diligent about staying on top of these numbers as deals move from stage to stage. Using a good customer relationship management (CRM) tool should help you to keep tabs on the health of your pipeline. See Chapter 10 for suggestions on CRM platforms.

QUALIFYING LEADS

At the end of the day, all selling starts with leads, which is why outbound selling, along with a good lead generation and prospecting process, is so important. Keep in mind the following:

- More leads at the top of the pipeline will result in better numbers at the bottom.
- Targeted leads at the top of the pipeline will provide better, faster results. These targeted leads are also known as your "low-hanging fruit."

Aaron Ross, who created the outbound sales model at Salesforce, talks about the various targeted lead types in the highly recommended and best-selling book, *Predictable Revenue*, which he coauthored with Mary Lou Tyler. In this book, he breaks down these leads into three categories: "Seeds," "Nets," and "Spears."

To quote Aaron:

- "*Seeds* are word-of-mouth leads, usually from prior relationships or happy customers. These are how companies get started and where most of your first customers come from.
  - "*Pros:* Highly profitable, word-of-mouth leads are the fastest to close and have the highest win rates. There's nothing better!

- *"Cons:* It's almost impossible to proactively grow them. You just have to do your best and be patient.

- *"Nets* are your marketing leads, such as internet marketing, events, webinars, white papers, advertising, and the like. You're casting a wide net, so this is about quantity over quality.

  - *"Pros:* Easy to generate. Some kinds of marketing programs are scalable, you can generate leads from everlasting content, and they are highly measurable. There are ways to generate leads at almost no cost.

  - *"Cons:* Not sure what will work, most leads aren't a fit, low conversion rates, mostly individuals/small businesses, small order sizes, a lot of cost and effort to build, optimize, and maintain.

- *"Spears* are when you have salespeople or business development people reaching out to specific targets, lists, or kinds of companies. It's a specific, targeted approach, driven by a human, with a goal of quality over quantity (the reverse of marketing Nets) . . . To be effective and scalable, you need a team of dedicated reps who only prospect—they don't close, manage accounts, or respond to inbound leads.

  - *"Pros:* Very predictable results, enables a very targeted approach to ideal prospects at executive levels, fast is-it-working-or-not feedback cycle, creates a pool of sales talent.

  - *"Cons:* Not profitable for small deals or customers, hard for old school companies to get the culture right (must avoid boiler room mentality), may be hard to get executive commitment to specialize and hire dedicated prospectors."

Good targeted leads provide you with a good start, but achieving success is all about how you guide those targeted leads through your pipeline. Look to design a streamlined process, which will act as lubrication for your pipeline. This lubrication consists of automation and acceleration tools, outsourced help, and all sorts of tactical and strategic sales hacks to speed things up.

A good sales process is a science, and science is the new art.

WHAT'S YOUR SALES STACK?

Developers and marketers have had their sales stacks for years. Developers have the benefit of being able to build their own sales stacks, and marketing has been fairly technical about building them for quite a few years. Finally, there are now enough sales tools for salespeople to build their own sales stack.

The great thing about these new tools is that they connect in various ways. I use a series of application program interface (API) integrations, manual virtual assistant work, and spreadsheets to piece it all together. You can think of your sales stack as your sales tool kit.

Figure 1.2 shows what a sales stack can look like:

SALES STACK

SCRAPING LISTS

CONTACT INFO

OUTBOUND E-MAIL

CRM

LEAD RESEARCH

DEMOS

PROPOSALS

CONTRACT

Figure 1.2   Sales Stack Funnel

Now, there are many different ways to build a sales stack and plenty of tools you can take advantage of for each piece of the pipeline. Some of the tools I'll mention in this book do very similar things, but you don't have to use just one tool. For example, I use multiple e-mail and messaging tools in my sales stack.

I recommend that you find the best subset of tools for your business, making sure to be diligent about connecting them properly. You can try using such integration tools as Zapier, IFTTT, or Bedrock Data if you need help. The less you have to do manually, the more efficient you will be.

As Wade Foster, the chief executive officer (CEO) of Zapier notes, "In a modern sales organization, leads and lead data span multiple applications. Being able to properly integrate the tools used to work a sales pipeline from start to finish is a must."

At the end of the day, you can have all of the technology in the world, but if you don't know how to use it, you're not going to get very far.

Now that we've got that out of the way, let's get into the good stuff.

CHAPTER **2**

List Building: Part 1

Finding and Defining Your Ideal Customer Profile

Building strong lists to generate leads at the top of your pipeline is arguably the most important part of the sales process. Without leads or "Nets," as Aaron Ross calls them, you have nothing. So start where your customers are. This is also called finding your ideal customer profile (ICP). Your ICP is a prospect who will most likely and most easily enter into a transaction or a business relationship with you.

To get started, ask yourself the following questions:

- What products are my customers using that I compete with, complement, or could translate into interest in my product? Following are two examples:
  - If you have a MailChimp-style service, you want to speak to MailChimp customers.
  - If potential customers are running Facebook Ads, they might also be interested in ad optimization or analytics software.
- Where are these potential customers living on the Web? Following are two examples:
  - Someone interested in your e-commerce service might have a store hosted on Shopify or built with Magento.

- If you want to find people to create a course online, find people who have already created content for that subject in book form and are selling it on Amazon. Then convince them to try adding video content.
- Which potential customers do I consider my low-hanging fruit?
  - The people already doing what you want them to do, just somewhere else.
  - Someone buying or selling a service on Craigslist that your company provides. It's easier to get the person to use you through Craigslist than to create a new buyer/seller from scratch. Pinterest has emerged as another way to source potential customers who are already buying or selling a service.
  - You're going after a potential buyer's budget that is focused on advertising, and you see that the potential buyer has a testimonial on a competing company's website. You know that the potential buyer has a budget and is already spending it somewhere else. Now it's time to get your slice of the pie—or even the whole pie!
- What can I decipher from my previous closed deals that I can use in new ones?
  - You keep closing deals with companies, so take a moment to ask yourself what these companies have in common and how you can apply these common variables when you are speaking to companies with the same common variables?

When my business was recruiting instructors to create courses on Udemy, my salespeople wouldn't have been successful if we hadn't relentlessly worked on nailing our ICP. To sell an expert on making money by teaching an online course, what did we look for?

First, we looked for people who were teaching a top programming language. Technology was our first concern—more specifically, Web development. So the first thing we did was take a look at the top-selling Web development books on Amazon. Our list was ranked in the same order as the best-selling programming language books.

The next most important thing was to see if these technology experts had prerecorded content, which meant that they could create a course faster than others who didn't understand video.

Lastly, we wanted to see which instructors had the most followers on social media. This meant that they could promote the course substantially.

These three things connected to create our ICP. A Ruby on Rails (programming language) instructor with high-quality educational You-Tube videos and 10,000 Twitter followers was a top target.

Some good places to look for information about potential buyers are the following:

- LinkedIn and Facebook groups
- Meetup, a network of local groups
- Industry conference websites
- Trade association forums and directories
- Job boards like Indeed, LinkedIn, and so forth
- Public legal filings
- CrunchBase, a website for discovering innovative companies and the people behind them
- AngelList, a U.S. website for start-ups
- Glassdoor, a jobs and recruiting website
- Yelp, a website that connects people with local businesses
- Shopify, a website for setting up an online store
- Etsy, a website for selling handmade, vintage, or craft items
- Kickstarter, a website that is the world's largest funding plat-form for creative projects
- Any company database or marketplace

To compile all of these ideal customers, you'll need some technical help.

EASY, NONTECHNICAL WEB SCRAPING

Web scraping is an essential hacking tactic to mine information on the Internet and to pull together an extensive, highly customized list of leads. Two pieces of software that I like to use for scraping lists off the Internet are Import.io and Kimono Labs. Since I am not a developer, I need to take advantage of tools that allow me to scrape the Web without writing any code, and that's what these tools do. If you have a developer on staff with some free time (but how often does that happen?), by all means, have that person build you a scraper with more functionality. For most sales hackers, either of these tools is all you need.

Import.io

Import.io can be used at the beginning of the sales process, when you're generating a large number of leads. It is important that, as an organization, you have a product market fit and that your sales or marketing team can clearly articulate what a target customer looks like so that they can know where to find information about that target customer on the Web.

Import.io is a general platform for accessing data on the Web without writing any code. It was not specifically designed for lead generation. Nevertheless, advanced sales and marketing people discovered the technology, started using it for lead generation, and began writing about the success that they were having. Lead generation is a perfect use of the technology.

For simply getting data into an ordered, usable format, Google Sheets is a great tool to use in conjunction with Import.io. In addition, data extracted from the Web using Import.io can also be imported into Salesforce or any other lead management or sales pipeline software.

Import.io Use Case Study   Andrew Fogg, chief data officer at Import.io, explains how to use the Import.io software:

> This approach was developed by some of Import.io's earliest users, and it is both ingenious and simple:
>
> Find a website where your ideal user can be found.

Build an API to that website (using Import.io, naturally) and extract as much data about each lead as you can.

Pull that data into a spreadsheet.

That's it. Three simple steps and it takes about 10 minutes, after which you will have thousands of quality leads to work with.

Now let's look at each of those steps in a bit more detail. To help you visualize how this can work for your business, I'm going to walk you through an example. Let's imagine that I'm in commercial real estate and want to talk to real estate brokers.

Step 1: Find your ideal user

The first step will require a little bit of imagination and thinking on your part. Where your ideal user can be found of course depends on who that person is. You'll probably need to spend some time getting to know your users and looking around the web to see where they hang out. Is it a forum? A professional association? Are they on social media?

The key here is to be as specific as possible when defining your ideal user (lead). The more specific you are, the more targeted your messaging can be. In our real estate example, I am going to use a real estate listing site in New York City. If I click through to one of those properties I can see the broker's name, e-mail (as a link from his name), and phone number—that's the data I'm after!

Steps 2 and 3: Extract the data and get it in a spreadsheet

I've combined steps 2 and 3 together here, because they are closely tied to the same process.

To get this data I could use a number of different options. The simplest way to do this is to build a Crawler, which will then go to each part of the site and pull data from all the pages that match the ones I train it on. This means I will end up with a big list of names and contact information, which I can export into Excel, CSV, or Google Sheets.

That's great, but Crawlers only create static data sets, which means that to get new data from this site I would have to re-crawl the whole site—and that would take a while.

Instead, I can do something a tad more complicated by building an *Extractor* to one page. Then I use the URL pattern of that page to generate all the other URLs for that site and use this batch search Google Sheet to pass all of those URLs through the Extractor. This has the benefit of being able to quickly refresh whenever I need to.

A quick note about getting the e-mail addresses: you'll notice, if you visit the page, that the e-mail address is displayed as a link to the estate agent's name. When I map this data, I need to make sure I map it as a link. It may look like I've only mapped his name, but when I export the data into Excel or Google Sheets, I will get one column with his name and another column with the text of the link—in this case his e-mail address.

In this particular example, I would also need to do a bit of data cleansing, because many of the properties are being sold by the same real estate agent so I am likely to end up with a lot of duplicates. This is easily done in either Excel/Google Sheets or most mass e-mailing software like MailChimp.

Depending on your ideal customer profile, these tools may only help you get a portion of the lists you need to build, but they're a good start. This information can be used as a springboard to get the rest of the list built quickly using the tools found in the next chapters. If you don't get contact information, as in the real estate example, you'll be able to use the information you do get to find the rest of the information later on.

DEEPER INSIGHTS INTO YOUR COMPETITORS' CUSTOMERS

Keeping tabs on your competitors and their customers is an essential strategy for filling your pipeline. When you're looking for the low-hanging fruit, the following services make it easy for you to go after buyers who are already using competing or complementary products. For example, if your service is marketing automation, then MailChimp, Marketo, HubSpot, and other marketing automation solution's users fit into your ICP, so you should use one of these services to go after potential customers. It's up to you to turn them into new customers.

Datanyze

Datanyze fits into the first half of the sales cycle by helping sales development reps (SDRs) find more opportunities. Using the Datanyze platform, sales reps can uncover new high-potential companies to reach out to, find the right contacts, and get their e-mail addresses—all in one shot.

Outside of sales prospecting, a lot of companies use Datanyze to retain their own customers. Customer success teams can be notified the day one of their customers has added a competitor's technology. This enables them to reach out to that customer before it's too late.

Datanyze integrates with Salesforce and syncs their technology and company data with any or all lead, account, contact, and opportunity records. This helps sales reps quickly identify which prospects are worth reaching out to within their Salesforce account.

Ilya Semin, chief executive officer (CEO) of Datanyze, says:

> Personalization is everything when doing outreach. Don't just reach out to a prospect that uses a competitor and say you have a similar product. Address your key differentiators and show them that you're willing to go the extra mile to get their attention.

Datanyze Use Case Study Kissmetrics's sales reps use Datanyze Alerts to receive a daily summary of every website that has dropped a competitor's technology or has added a technology that integrates with KISSmetrics. This enables them to get in touch with prospective customers who have a high potential to purchase their product. These are key buying signals that allow the sales reps to act quickly. Wouldn't you like to know when a customer has signed up with a competitor?

BuiltWith

BuiltWith, a website profiler tool, allows you to see all websites that are using certain Web-based services or integrations so that you can easily create lead lists with the information.

Start creating your lead list by choosing the technology you're interested in. BuiltWith will come back with a list of all the sites on the Internet that use your chosen technology.

You can then customize your list by sorting and filtering as much as you need. The options for filtering your list include (but are not limited to) the following:

- Location—down to a postal address and zip code
- Traffic ranking
- People—names and titles of people at the business
- Company names
- Vertical—shopping/forums/software
- Top-level domain (TLD)—for example, .com .uk .de
- Telephone numbers
- E-mail addresses
- Other technologies—find websites in your lead list that are using particular premium technologies

BuiltWith also allows you to get actual names, titles, and e-mails of people at companies. BuiltWith claims to have over seven years of historical data, and it has built a comprehensive contact and e-mail list that provides users with the ability to see qualified e-mails for businesses for which they've found titles and known e-mail addresses.

If you sign up for a paid plan, BuiltWith will pass its technology data into your Salesforce account so that you can further qualify your leads.

BuiltWith Use Case Study   J. Ryan Williams leads the sales development rep (SDR) team at AdRoll and was one of its first sales reps back in 2011. An integral part of AdRoll's sales growth was due to its clever use of BuiltWith's services. AdRoll knew its ICP was e-commerce stores, so J. Ryan Williams used BuiltWith to tell him which sites were built using Magento. Magento is an e-commerce software platform that allows shop owners to quickly build a store online.

Other options to check out are iDataLabs, MixRank, and SimilarWeb.

TARGETING KEY EXECUTIVES, INFLUENCERS, AND HIGH-POTENTIAL BUYERS

In some cases, you'll want to focus your competitive research tactics on an individual key player. Try the following options to target that key player based on social media, and add them to your lists.

Followerwonk

Followerwonk is an analytics tool on Twitter. It has many features, but one of its most popular uses for business is "audience targeting."

By analyzing the top followers of any brand, or even your competitors' brands, you can find highly qualified prospects, leads, or engagement opportunities. Followerwonk calculates the "Social Authority" of each Twitter account, so you can sort by the most influential people in each space.

Followerwonk Use Case Study At Udemy, we used Followerwonk to target people with certain words in their bios. If we wanted to find PHP (Hypertext Preprocessor) experts to teach a programming course, we could use the bio search function to search Twitter bios for PHP experts. It was a great way for us to engage with and understand the players in the space.

The best part was that we could sort by the number of followers the PHP experts had and go after the ones with the biggest reach. Getting content on board was a win, but getting someone with a preexisting audience was an even bigger win, as they would likely target that audience and turn them into Udemy students.

Little Bird

Little Bird helps you find influencers by using certain keywords, seeing which potential buyers to connect with, and seeing who's connecting with your competitors. Similar to Followerwonk, you can easily use Little Bird to search Twitter for potential buyers based on criteria that you create, such as company, location, follow count, keywords, and so on.

Little Bird can actually be used in many stages of the sales process. It can be used in the lead research stage, when you are preparing for a sales call. Maybe you'd like to understand a business's ecosystem and the people who influence it. The Little Bird team itself uses the product to identify the people, publications, and businesses that matter in order to understand the space and players better on the initial discovery call. With this data in hand, the team has been able to turn twice as many leads into sales opportunities.

Little Bird also can be used in the lead nurturing stage. By using the Share and Engage feature, you can monitor trends in the space and leverage the information before other people do. You'll be positioned as the expert, be more consultative in your sale, and take the competitive advantage in the deal.

With Little Bird's application program interface (API), you can pull data out of existing customer relationship management (CRM) systems, enter it into Little Bird, and identify the influencers that cross multiple customer and prospect databases. This helps you and your marketing organization prioritize your efforts on relationship building.

At this point, you should have a pretty good idea of how to figure out which companies you'd like to target. Now it's time to build these lists into usable account databases.

CHAPTER 3

List Building: Part 2

Defining Your Total Addressable Market (TAM)

A uthor's note: The following section is written with help from my friend and colleague, Daniel Barber, vice president of revenue at Node.io.

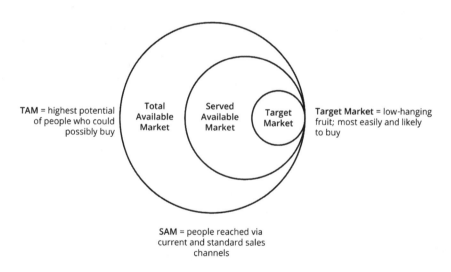

TAM = highest potential of people who could possibly buy

Total Available Market

Served Available Market

Target Market

Target Market = low-hanging fruit; most easily and likely to buy

SAM = people reached via current and standard sales channels

Figure 3.1   Total Addressable Market (TAM), Served Available Market (SAM), and Target Market (TM)

Whether you're selling for a start-up or an enterprise, you need a realistic and specific idea of your true revenue opportunity. Once you understand the profile of your customer, you should determine your total addressable market (TAM), which measures the total of potential customers you can sell to.

If you sell point-of-sales systems or digital cash registers that work with American banks, your TAM is every small business in the United States of America.

If you sell sales e-mail automation software, your TAM is everyone who uses e-mail in his or her sales process. You can cross-reference customer relationship management (CRM) users with Outlook or Gmail users to find a massive audience of potential customers.

ENRICH *YOUR* CUSTOMERS

To find your company's TAM, you want to determine how deep the market is for companies with a similar background. Taking a step back and looking at their customer base will inform you of outlying trends that could support a move into a new industry or market segment.

Tapping into the commonalities across your customer base will leverage enormous value and build a more complete picture of your customers.

Map your customer base, using a tiered data framework.

Tier 1: Sales Cycle, Average Contract Value (ACV), Win Rate

The goal of Tier 1 is to understand the sales velocity (i.e., the number of opportunities multiplied by the ACV, multiplied by the win rate, divided by the sales cycle) of your customer base.

- These data points will form the basic foundation and expose any outliers in the customer data.
- Invest time to validate the integrity of your data.

Tier 2: Industry (and Vertical), Employee Size, Growth Score, Location, and Technology Stack

The goal of Tier 2 is to add an additional layer of firmographic data that will form the basis for your size and scope analysis.

- There are a number of large data sources to validate industry, vertical, employee size, growth score, and location, including Mattermark, FactSet, and Hoover's. When you are evaluating your potential database partner, use the following criteria to help guide your choice:

  - Matching percentage (i.e., number of your customers that are present in the list)

  - Number of additional data (commonalities) points

  - Data integrity—check third-party sources to validate

- Industry and vertical are interdependent (and often confused). An example of the relationship is that Box is in the *cloud storage* vertical within the *technology* industry.

- If your customers have adopted a set of technologies, surfacing this data at scale will provide an additional proxy. For the technology stack, there are several sources to capture this data: Datanyze, Ghostery Enterprise, BuiltWith, and SimilarWeb. Using these providers will help you determine if your customers are using website analytics, marketing automation, Pay Per Click advertising, A/B testing, and so forth.

Tier 3: Company Specific Data

- By using freelancers (from Upwork, CrowdFlower, etc.), you can add valuable data from your competitors' websites, the AppExchange, or any website. If you have a hypothesis that you'd like to test (e.g., your buyer is a vice president of marketing), you can have the freelancers do a pass against your customer list via LinkedIn.

- The scope of this collection is broad, so identify a few hypotheses, and then you can validate them from your Tier 1 data points.

MEET YOUR FUTURE CUSTOMERS

Once you've collected extensive data on your *existing* customers, it's time to turn them into your *future* customers. Assuming you've invested in one of the databases mentioned earlier, this process will be fairly straightforward.

This next set of steps will draw on your customer list and extrapolate the data across the data set of your database partner.

Step 1: Map Your Customer Data

1. Using Excel, create a data sheet for each *Tier*.

2. Form a consistent list of your customers across each data sheet.

3. Cluster (and sort) the companies with high concentration across each variable, specifically those that perform well across the Tier 1 data points.

Step 2: Identify the Early Adopters and Mainstream (see Geoffrey Moore's Crossing the Chasm)

Place your customers into two buckets:

1. Those that have a high number of variables and high-performing characteristics from Tier 1. Companies that are early adopters and have a faster than average sales velocity will surface on this list.

2. Those that are outside your (assumed) ideal customer profile (ICP) but possess high-performing characteristics from Tier 1. This list will provide companies that have a faster than average sales velocity but may not be in your present ICP.

Step 3: Validate the Size and Scope

1. Based on your two customer data sets, use the confirmed variables to export companies from the largest database available for your given industry and set of verticals.

2. Separate the two distinct buckets (from Step 2) to ensure that you can test the performance of each data set.

MAKE IT ACTIONABLE

Now that you've collected all of this data, what should you do with it? The answer is: provide the sales team with the same insights that you've collected.

Step 1: Confirm the Variables

When you check the weather, are you interested in the barometric pressure? Probably not, so apply the same logic to the data fields that you have collected. The goal in Step 1 is to understand the optimal information that can be effectively positioned to personalize the team's outreach.

1. Take a holistic approach to how the team can use this data:
   - Industry/vertical will align future customers (see Geoffrey Moore: "Bowling Pin Strategy").
   - Geographical concentration adds degrees of separation and can be valuable for marketing events.
   - Technology providers will allow easy dynamic fields within e-mails.
   - Competitive takeaways will provide great talking points.
2. Limit the variables to four to five (to avoid paralysis by analysis).
3. Choose your filters (for the Dashboard) so that you have overarching segmentation.

Step 2: Create Custom Fields within the CRM System

Add a collection of custom fields, and be particular about how you present the data (i.e., on the account record and/or the contact record). This will involve using a feedback loop with the sales team around what they would find valuable—that is, specific to the sales process.

Step 3: Mapping the Fields to Reports in Salesforce

In Step 3, you want to think about the optimal method for presenting the data so that (1) the sales team can quickly interpret the chart and (2) you are telling a story with each data point.

My advice is to use a combination of different charts and leverage feedback from the sales team on how they interpret each report. The longer it takes for individuals to understand the context of the report, the less valuable the report is.

REFINE AND OPTIMIZE THE ENTIRE PROCESS

Finding your ICP will ensure that you are having the *right* conversations. Defining your TAM will uncover the breadth and depth of your market. These two exercises are not designed to be "set-and-forget." As your customer evolves and you test your outliers, you'll need to tweak and adjust the model.

In order to create and maintain this process, you should have a qualitative feedback loop from your customer success/account management team and a quantitative feedback loop to continually improve the ICP and TAM.

COMPANY DATABASES

There are plenty of databases out there for you to use in order to inquire about companies. Things to look for might include the following:

- Amount of money the company has raised to date
- Timing of last round raised
- Employee head count
- New employees recently hired
- Job titles and new titles added
- Company headquarters
- Public relations (PR) announcements, new product launches, funding, key hires, or partnerships

- Legal filings
- Growth rate (revenue, funding, head count)

This is also how you tell your "whales" from your "fish" and the difference between who is ready to buy and who is not. Again, keep refining your ICP and TAM until you have a core audience or perfect profile. Low-hanging fruit can be your easy, wide-open layups. You just need to know what they look like.

Let's get into some of your best options for using company information databases.

CrunchBase and AngelList

CrunchBase and AngelList are your free and simple sources for gathering the information you need on technology companies from pre-seed to post-IPO (initial public offering) to exit. Both CrunchBase and AngelList have application program interfaces (APIs) that you can use, which are good but still somewhat limited, as they don't want you to rip off their entire database. If you're somewhat technical in basic Ruby on Rails or Python, or you think you can learn quickly, check out the blog posts of Chief Operating Officer (COO) of Scripted, Ryan Buckley, on Scraping CrunchBase.

If you're not too technical, you can use the nontechnical Web-scraping tools that were previously mentioned (Import.io and Kimono Labs) to scrape the information you require. Supplement this with virtual assistants, and you'll have everything you need to start building massive lists in one shot.

Glassdoor is also a good place to get company data.

Owler

Owler is like a souped-up version of CrunchBase, with a better ability to sort companies, get alerts, and surface information more clearly.

In Owler, you can sort by funding, acquisitions, or leadership changes, or you can visit a company page and see all of its competitors.

Owler provides data and profiles on over 10,000 private and public companies, but the key features are its alerts and snapshots. Get weekly competitive intelligence reports on data comparisons that include information on the following:

- Chief executive officers (CEOs)
- Revenue
- Press releases
- Blog posts
- Social media statistics
- Competitive set
- And more

Mattermark

Mattermark offers a way of sourcing, analyzing, and tracking private companies around the world. By using the wealth of data that Mattermark has gathered on companies, using proprietary information such as a "Growth Score" or "Mindshare Score" allows business-to-business (B2B) sales professionals to identify more readily potential private companies they would like to do business with.

Mattermark provides a feed into any user's instance of Salesforce, giving the user the ability to leverage the data in his or her CRM system. You can connect your LinkedIn account to see how your first-level connections are connected to the people in the private companies you have identified on Mattermark. This is a great way of getting warm introductions to these private firms.

For even more records that are both private and public, check out PitchBook VC and S&P Capital IQ.

Socedo

Socedo allows you to pick conversations, keywords, hashtags, and handles to track prospects. Just set up search criteria for each prospect, and Socedo selects accounts across Twitter that might be relevant to you. Then you approve the prospects it has selected.

Once you have your list of prospects, Socedo favorites a recent tweet of the propect's. An hour later, Socedo follows the prospect. When the prospect follows you back, Socedo sends you a direct message using the prospect's first name, a reference to the prospect's tweet, and a Call to Action (CTA). This CTA is trackable, and the entire flow, including the direct message, is customizable.

CEO of Socedo, Aseem Badshah, adds:

> It's important to spend time coming up with some really good keywords that will help you find your target customers. Think about what they are tweeting about instead of what you or your competitors are tweeting about. What events do they attend? Who do they retweet? What do they read? The prospect search criteria takes some time, but it is crucial to your success no matter how you prospect.

You've done a great job on gathering lists of companies. The next step is figuring out the right way in the door.

CHAPTER 4

List Building: Part 3

Getting in the Door

Once you've done your work on finding the right companies, you need to find the right person to get you in the door. This can be simplified in a manner that is similar to how we found the right companies.

TOP-DOWN AND BOTTOM-UP TARGETING

The next step is finding out who in the organization you'll need to target. For some industries, it's a no-brainer. Are you selling in the digital advertising field? You probably can derive from the market that you'll need to talk to the vice president or manager of digital marketing. Are you selling sponsorships to in-person events? You can probably aim directly for the field marketing manager.

These are your ideal customer profiles. If you're starting a business from scratch, the next step is a bit harder. If you can't immediately figure this out, you'll employ either top-down or bottom-up targeting.

Top-Down Targeting

Aim for the highest person in marketing in the organization whom you can find. If it's someone in marketing you want to speak with, but you don't know who, then reach out to the vice president (VP) of marketing or the chief marketing officer (CMO). You should *very* briefly introduce your product or product area and then ask to be introduced to the appropriate person. Below is an example of such an e-mail.

27

Subject: Appropriate Person
> Or Subject: Referral Request
> Hi [First name],
> I see you work at [company] and was wondering if you could put me in touch with the person responsible for [X product value].
> Many thanks for your help,
> [Your name]

A last-ditch effort can be made to reach out to the chief executive officer (CEO), but it's best to start with the highest person on that individual silo within the company.

This tends to work for two reasons:

1. The person you are e-mailing is not responding to you; the person is introducing you to someone who will. The work on this person's part is minimal. Make the e-mail very short and to the point. The point is getting the introduction, not pitching the product.

2. When the recipient receives the introduction, it's coming from the recipient's boss. Usually if the boss tells the recipient to do something, he or she will do it and won't even ask for context most of the time.

This tactic and e-mailing have been used widely, so be aware that they may be losing their effectiveness. This tactic also is not very empathetic. You'll need to find ways to be more creative when using the top-down targeting approach. We'll dive into this topic in more detail in Chapter 8, "Outbound E-Mailing and Messaging."

Bottom-Up Targeting

If the organization is large, you can come at it from a different angle. Lists are so easy to build these days that it's worth sending a couple of templated e-mails. This approach only works if you have a product that would be used company-wide or with somewhat junior people, like in software sales. If it's a product like Domo, a business management platform made for the CEO, it's probably not going to work.

Start by targeting a few junior employees and selling them on the fact that they can be champions for the product. They'll out-perform their peers, and when their boss asks how, they can plug the product to the team as the fastest way to earn a raise or promotion.

Farlan Dowell, head VP of sales at Rainforest QA, spoke about this at a recent Sales Hacker Series event. He calls this the act of "becoming a hero maker," meaning make the internal champion a hero by being the guy who brings on the amazing new product and proves it out for the team.

You can think of bottom-up targeting almost like entering a parasite that infects the rest of the organization. I've heard sales reps say things to their bosses like, "If the company doesn't pay for this, I'll come out of pocket and buy a one-seat license myself." In this case, the sales rep knows that it's helping her or him close deals, hit quotas, and make more money. If it costs the sales rep $39 per month out of pocket, it's definitely worth it.

If you can do a good job at turning these reps into your buying champions, the odds are that you'll have the full attention of the right decision maker in no time. It's a lot easier to get these junior employees started on free trials than it is to get in immediately with the VP.

Figure 4.1 Targeting Strategies

LinkedIn Sales Navigator

I had a premium LinkedIn Sales Plus account and recently moved over to the LinkedIn Sales Navigator account. I use LinkedIn to get insights on company information and then to drill deep into job titles and employee backgrounds. For example, it would be great to be able to quickly find the profiles of all employees who are at the director level, are in sales, have been more than four years with the company, and are located in Dublin.

LinkedIn Sales Navigator finally gives you, the LinkedIn user, an experience that those who are involved in sales prospecting have been looking for. I have a team of virtual assistants who do my LinkedIn sales prospecting for me based on the direction I provide them, and this new format of lead searching should increase their numbers dramatically.

Another new feature is adding potential targets to a leads list, as opposed to starring the contact as you would have previously on LinkedIn. Once there, you can go back and InMail them or export their e-mail using Datanyze or Salesloft and then contact them in multiple different ways over time.

LinkedIn is still the number one source for up-to-date information, so these new features go a long way toward making it easier to search and sort through it all. I don't know why LinkedIn didn't do it sooner. It's just one more step in LinkedIn's march to become your one and only customer relationship management (CRM) tool.

A few other companies go even further technologically to help you connect with your ideal customer profile (ICP).

Node.io

Node.io understands and triangulates the relationships between people, companies, and keywords on the Web, with the goal of connecting interested parties. They do this through an account-based sales intelligence platform that acts as a personal sales analyst, recommending which accounts to break into, which contacts at those accounts to engage, and personalized account plans with guidance on how to close.

DataFox

DataFox enables the creation of targeted lead lists with accurate buyer contact information through suggestions of new companies that resemble your best customers and the surfacing of conferences attended by your prospects, and then DataFox alerts you when new prospects enter your territory.

DataFox provides highly curated and customized buying signals—such as new patents filed, office openings, Security and Exchange Commission (SEC) document filings and management changes—for an entire territory in real time. These customized buying signals help hunters and existing account managers with large account bases to prioritize accounts that are more likely to buy and focus conversations on the pain points that customers care about, increasing cross-sell revenue while reducing the time taken to run through the deal cycle.

Sales reps can use DataFox inside Salesforce as part of their day-to-day work flow or through the DataFox user interface (UI).

Growbots

Growbots allows you to set up targets based on criteria such as market vertical, location, size, Web traffic, technologies used by the company, and job title. For example, Growbots can search for CEOs of San Francisco software companies with 11–50 employees who use HubSpot. Growbots is among the 1 million highest trafficked websites on the Internet.

Growbot's tool automatically gives you a list of people matching criteria with verified e-mails, and all contacts are de-duplicated with your CRM system, meaning that you only get prospects you never contacted.

Spiderbook

Spiderbook helps identify prospects and leads, and lives in your sales stack pre-CRM. Other than using Spiderbook for lead generation, you can also use it to identify companies that will partner with you in the sales process, people to use for references, and what your competitive landscape looks like.

Spiderbook takes your seed information, such as current customers, partners, suppliers, and product profiles, and matches it with customers online. Aman Naimat, CEO of Spiderbook, says:

> No matter how good the leads are that we generate, you still need a four- to eight-touch sales process that is efficient and personalized. Even the perfect lead will fail if you don't follow a rigorous process and don't utilize relevant content to personalize the messaging.

RainKing

RainKing is a database that surfaces not only information about potential buyers but also details on when they're supposed to buy and how much money they have to spend. For example, RainKing can provide a public report that says how much a large company will spend on CRM in the next 6–12 months and what type of budget it has to spend on CRM. This is super valuable information if you're selling CRM systems.

LEAN ON YOUR INDUSTRY ALLIES

Lean on your existing network to make contacts. Again, if you've already landed a few deals, this makes things a lot easier. My advice is to segment your past deals based on company size or deal size, and see if there are any common paths you've navigated within the organizational chart of those companies. Going through past deals allows you to figure out who you might have spoken to at a similar organization and then gives you a potential job title to look out for at the new target company.

You can also reach out to, or make friends at, companies that are selling their products to similar companies but are not your competitors.

Recently, I had the pleasure of meeting with the founder of VideoGenie, Justin Nassiri, and his first salesperson, Jake. They weren't sure who to target in their outreach to Fortune 1000 companies. They had no past data to look through, as these would be their first big accounts. I received an introduction to Justin and Jake from the team at SocialChorus and recognized that they were selling to a similar market but with very different and noncompeting products. I recommended that the two teams share contacts for accounts, because it would be a win-win-win situation. Don't be afraid to contact the peers in your industry to ask for help.

SellerCrowd

SellerCrowd is an anonymous forum that allows people in advertising technology to exchange information to target companies and accounts. For example, if you're looking to sell digital media to Nike, you can ask the forum whom you should speak to at Nike. You should get back an informational response. You may even get contact information. We're still waiting for someone to do this for SaaS (software as a service)—could it be you?

Using Twitter to Generate Warm Leads

Industry experts began using the term *social selling* when social media became big and salespeople who adjusted and embraced social media became masters of generating new leads.

Now there's a new tool out there that automates most of this.

Socedo

Socedo integrates directly with Marketo and Salesforce to track leads that are generated from social media further down the pipeline. Socedo also recommends using a social media management tool like Buffer, Hootsuite, or Sprout Social to track conversations.

The team at Tallwave, for example, is using Socedo with an individual business development representative to look for start-up founders on Twitter and then is using the automated messaging to ask if the prospect is interested in sharing more about his or her business. From there a call is set up, and the representative can fill his or her day with qualified warm sales calls. The reps are setting up meetings this way more than through their outbound e-mail campaigns.

Visit www.SalesHacker.com/library for more information on finding your total addressable market (TAM), ICP, and contact list building.

CHAPTER 5

Uncovering Contact Information

By now, you have all of the information you could possibly need to build highly targeted lists of potential buyers. You have potential targets at all levels within the companies—ideal customer profiles (ICPs), both top-down and bottom-up. You have company names, job titles, and other attributes. The only thing you're missing now is your potential targets' contact information, which is a very important piece of the puzzle.

REMOVE DUPLICATES EARLY ON

Before you start gathering contact information, you should build up a number of lists from sources across the Internet, using the tactics from previous chapters in this book. Once you have these lists, it's likely you will have a handful of duplicates. Don't waste time or resources gathering e-mail addresses for the same people multiple times. Instead, quickly remove duplicates from your lists.

My favorite way to remove duplicates from my lists is to use Google Sheets. It recently released new add-ons that you can install easily from Google Sheets in the Google Chrome store. Just click Add-ons in the navigation bar, where File and Edit are, and find the add-on called Remove Duplicates. Once you have that add-on, put all of the sheets together on a master sheet. Then open Remove Duplicates, and run the program to delete duplicate cells.

If your lists are already segmented and you want to keep them separate, create a master sheet and run the program, but don't allow it to delete duplicate cells. Instead, ask the program to highlight the duplicate and the original cells in green, and then manually delete duplicates from one of the lists.

You also may want to check your current customer relationship management (CRM) system for accounts that you're already talking to. The process for doing this is different with all CRM systems, but you can usually pull a report, add it to the document, and remove duplicates (both from the original and from your CRM system). You won't need to find the e-mail addresses if you already have them, so it should save you some time and money.

All of these minor, trainable tasks are perfect assignments for a virtual assistant to handle. I'll get to that shortly.

Now you're ready to generate contact information. There's no secret way to do this. An e-mail address is number one. If you can get a direct phone number, that's good, too.

Toofr

Toofr is the best tool I've seen for finding business e-mail addresses and building a massive list of potential contacts, as long as you have a first name, a last name, and a domain name. Toofr can verify or find thousands of e-mails at a time. Just upload the CSV (comma separated values) file, and then retrieve the export file. This is important for lowering the bounce rate of e-mails that you send, which can set off spam triggers and mess up the effectiveness of your e-mail campaigns.

For example, let's say my goal is to contact the vice president (VP) of marketing at 200 target companies that have just closed Series B round of funding and are on CrunchBase. I can scrape the company information (first name, last name, domain) into a CSV file using the tools from earlier in this book and upload that neatly organized CSV file directly into Toofr. The final result should be a CSV file with verified e-mail addresses alongside the information I imported. The data comes from multiple sources and is usually double- or triple-verified, so it's quite accurate.

ZoomInfo

ZoomInfo is a software-as-a-service (SaaS) company that sells access to its database of information about businesspeople and companies to sales, marketing, and recruiting professionals. ZoomInfo has made a big comeback in my book. I used to think databases had some of the stalest leads because it was harder for them to stay up to date, but ZoomInfo is a whole new product with some of the most accurate contact information, especially direct dials.

Prospect.io

Prospect.io allows you to pull all contact information directly from Web pages. It's another way to scrape as much data from the Web as possible. All you do is type in a domain using the full URL (www.___.com) and click Go. It will pull all contact information from across the site as the internal crawler searches page by page. Prospect.io also has a bulk upload tool and an application program interface (API) for those requiring multiple domain look-ups.

PULLING CONTACT INFORMATION DIRECTLY FROM LINKEDIN

SalesLoft

SalesLoft, a sales development software company, is great for prospecting directly from LinkedIn, which means you have a target individual in mind and need his or her full contact information. I find that using SalesLoft is most helpful when I have a company name and a job title but I don't know the name of the person I'm looking for. By using LinkedIn's new Sales Navigator, I can now easily search LinkedIn for these contacts and simply export them using the SalesLoft Chrome extension. SalesLoft will show me my lists of exports and, by their best guess, the full contact information for my exported leads. SalesLoft's data is usually very accurate.

If all you have is a company name and a job title, searching can still be done a bit manually, but that's what you have virtual assistants for.

SalesLoft is getting away from this area of the business, but their services still work well.

Capture (by RingLead)

Capture is a wonderful new tool from RingLead that allows you to go to any site or social profile and pull data from it using a Chrome browser extension.

For example, you can visit a company's Team page and scrape all team members' names. This allows you to get their contact information and import it directly into Salesforce. The extension allows you to do this from websites, social media profiles, job listing sites, spreadsheets, Twitter lists, Google searches, and more.

Capture can even be used within Salesforce to keep existing data up to date or with existing external databases to update incomplete or stale data.

Datanyze also has a plug-in for this. Check out Ecquire, too. Velocify recently released a competing product in the space as well.

E-mail Verification and Enrichment

Once you've built massive e-mail lists from various data sources, be sure to do the following:

- Make sure the e-mails are verified and don't bounce back. High bounce rates can lead to blacklisted domains, which will send your e-mails to the recipients' spam folder. Bad e-mail addresses will also throw off your e-mail optimization efforts and ruin your conversion pipeline.

- Enrich the data you have so that you get a full lead profile that you can work with. This gives you a quick and easy way to turn an e-mail address into a full profile on the person.

BriteVerify

BriteVerify is a data verification service that can be used to verify data such as e-mail addresses, phone numbers, and mailing addresses. It is extremely simple and easy to use. Its service allows you to verify e-mails one-by-one or to upload lists to verify multiple e-mails all at once.

Its API is the best part. It allows you to connect your CRM, point of sales (POS) software, Web forms, or mobile applications so that any e-mail that comes in is automatically verified as soon as it enters your system.

Also check out Kickbox.io, which is another e-mail address verification service.

Clearbit

Clearbit is an easy-to-use enrichment tool with an API that you can pass a lead through, and it will tell you everything you need to know about that lead. You can pass numerous domain names or e-mail addresses through the API, and Clearbit will fill out a full profile based on that information.

Clearbit released a very good Google Docs plug-in that allows you to build lists right into the document without leaving your Google-based world.

Clearbit is a really good way to clean up new data, fill in the blanks, or keep data clean.

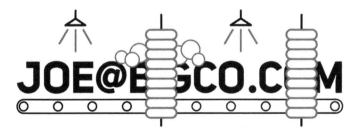

Figure 5.1   Data Enrichment

Whatever you do, don't skimp on making sure your data is clean and up to date. Sending e-mails to incorrect or expired e-mail addresses is worse than sending no e-mails. You can land your domain in spam folders, or worse, you can be locked out of your e-mail account by your e-mail provider.

CHAPTER 6

Lead Research

List building and lead research go hand in hand in the sales process. At this point, you have the tools to fully build your lists but not to put them into action. You still need to learn things about your prospects so that you can deliver a message that is relevant to them and provide value in the sales process. Better yet, you still need to know who you need to learn more about and segment your lists further. These are just two key reasons to research and prepare ahead of time.

There have been heated debates in many sales circles about the outbound sales process. Some people like to play a "spray-and-pray" game, in which they blast out e-mails, like the "appropriate person" e-mail I referred to in Chapter 4. Others like to show every prospect a certain level of personalization in an e-mail. Regardless of what you do, it all comes down to lead research, segmenting, and messaging. We'll dive deep into segmenting and messaging in the next two chapters, but for now let's talk about lead research.

When you are doing lead research, you'll want to find out as much information as possible on a company and individual contacts before you reach out to important prospects. Find triggers or action events to use as a reason to contact them.

Following are examples of trigger events that you can mention in your outreach.

Company

- Fund-raiser, liquidity event, acquisition, or company milestone
- New headquarters or expansion

- Key executive hire
- Good public relations (PR) (company's growth, product release, CEO appearing on *The Ellen Degeneres Show*, etc.)
- Good blog post
- Competitor's PR
- Awards or recognition
- New contracts or partnerships

Individual

- Job change
- Awards or recognition
- Good blog post

Twitter or social media trigger event (e.g., you'll know from Twitter if the person cares about a local sports team winning the Super Bowl).

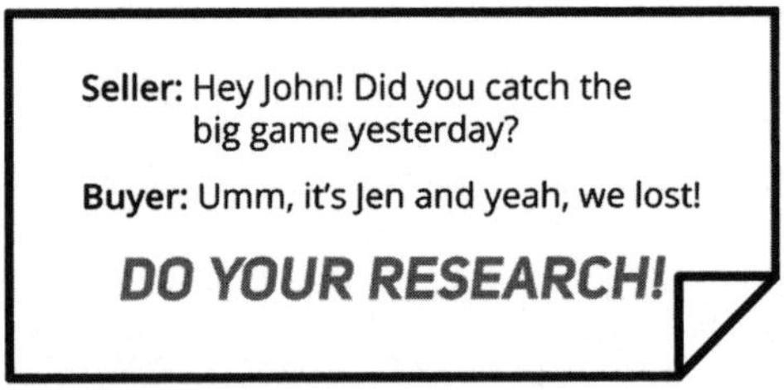

Figure 6.1 Split Research

There is data across the Internet, but uncovering it is the hard part. The Internet can be a massive "black hole," so you need a good way to sift through all of the information to find content that is relevant to your prospect's company. Many companies are solving this problem by using a mix of scraping, crawling, artificial intelligence, and big data analytics.

TRIGGER EVENT, ALERTS, AND RESEARCHING

InsideView

InsideView is one of the most robust tools when it comes to prospecting, and it continues to go wider and deeper. It's a great tool for keeping your data up to date by tracking what's happening within accounts across the Internet. It allows you to sort through its prospect database to track, and even contact, companies with relevant trigger events.

InsideView provides sales reps with updates on all business and social events that are happening for each prospect. This consists of notifications and daily e-mail alerts that are delivered directly to your inbox. InsideView can also provide a real-time dossier on every prospect in your customer relationship management (CRM) system; hence the phrase "CRM intelligence."

You can even use InsideView to figure out which connections in your network can introduce you to potential buyers who are on your list. This works through connected social networks and a company's internal employee networks.

FunnelFire

FunnelFire is an online sales intelligence platform that allows users to filter prospect-related online data. FunnelFire continuously tracks keywords across thousands of news sources. In normal use, this allows users to find relevant articles about industry topics to use in their sales process. Another way to use this data is to have FunnelFire identify companies mentioned in different ways and with different trigger events. Several customers use this data to help them identify new companies to target.

When their software combines this with e-mail alerts on trigger events, end users can be notified about new companies falling into particular trigger events and then use this information to find new leads.

A publicly traded company can use FunnelFire in several ways. On a daily basis, the marketing team gets inbound leads. These leads get pushed automatically into the team's CRM system. The CRM system automatically assigns the sales reps based on territory and a number of rules. Through the CRM system's integration, profiles on these new leads are generated in real-time. These profiles are compiled from thousands of data sources and profiles across the Internet, and a dossier is created instantaneously so that sales reps can gather information and assess the company in seconds.

Mark LaRosa, chief executive officer (CEO) of FunnelFire, adds:

> Most of the sales process has been completed by the time reps call on prospects. Prospects are more educated than ever, because data is everywhere. As a result, they expect sales reps to be just as educated.

DiscoverOrg

DiscoverOrg is a sales and marketing intelligence platform that is set apart by the fact that it employs a team that consistently dials into accounts to make sure its database information is fresh. DiscoverOrg almost acts as your pre-SDR (sales development rep), gathering company and market information, following trigger events and job changes, and figuring out an organization's structure and contact information.

DiscoverOrg integrates with many top CRM systems and even offers a browser extension for real-time use.

LINKEDIN ADVANCED SETTINGS AND SALES NAVIGATOR

LinkedIn Advanced Settings and Sales Navigator provide relevant content and news from your prospects, delivered to you in real time. This has worked well since LinkedIn's acquisition of Newsle, which had similar functionality.

If you're looking for something basic, you can always go the Google Alerts route.

Also, check out Birdhouse to get Twitter alerts on your Contacts and Accounts.

Figure 6.2 Job Alerts

Predictive Sales and Web Signaling

This area of the sales stack is a really interesting new wrinkle in the mix. The companies in this chapter are working on ways to take information from your past deals, your top keywords, public information, news, and other buying signals to create a web of potential buyers.

This is the power of the new era in sales. Salespeople never would have been able to see these potential leads in the past. Developers are bringing their expertise to our playing fields, and it's just getting interesting. The following tools allow you to see and capitalize on your lowest-hanging fruit.

Infer

Infer provides you with what is called "predictive lead scoring." Infer integrates with your data via CRM or marketing automation software to develop a customized list of buying signals that it can then use to find companies looking to buy from you. All you need is an e-mail address or company name, and Infer can build a robust buying profile for that lead.

Infer can also tell you which of your current marketing qualified leads (MQLs) you can consider more easily closable than other leads. Infer does this based on multiple factors that it gathers from public information, such as recent news, company size, new job openings, social media use, legal filings, and so forth.

Infer also uses the data from your CRM system and pairs it with machine learning so that, when you input a new lead, Infer can give you an accurate lead score based on past deal wins and losses.

Compile

Compile aggregates data from the Internet, including, among others, message board chatter, budget documents, security advisories, and news sites.

A natural language processor-based engine called the Autocurator sifts through the data to identify only those bits that indicate a potential sales opportunity. The engine identifies patterns that indicate a clear buying action.

For example, a technology road map presentation discussing a new citywide Wi-Fi network or a recent data breach at a global organization is a good indicator of a need for a specific product and would show up publicly across the Internet.

Using a trained set of known good and bad leads, the Autocurator assigns a score to each lead. Only those leads that display a clear buying trigger and strong relevance to your product are retained. These leads are then paired with the contact information of the buyers and pushed to the Compile dashboard, e-mail digest, or your CRM tool.

Other tools to check out in this category include Mintigo and MightySignal.

Use Your Network

There are a few solid products whose core business models are to provide you with the full use of your professional networks. This means that you can use your friends and colleagues to facilitate warm introductions, effectively speeding up deal cycles.

Conspire

By connecting your e-mail account and allowing it to analyze your e-mail data, Conspire understands who you know and how well you know them. With that understanding, Conspire finds the strongest path of connections in your extended network to the people and companies you are trying to reach.

Landing deals early at a start-up is difficult because potential customers don't know anything about the company. In such cases, a warm introduction is key to getting attention and, potentially, a meeting. Sales reps use Conspire to prioritize leads according to how strong an introduction they can get from their professional network (including current or former colleagues, friends, classmates, etc.) When the reps have strong paths, they are able to get meaningful introductions from people who know both the reps and the targets well. This means that the relationship with the potential customers starts with a high degree of trust.

Conspire is using data and science to understand the strength of connections between you and your friends, and your friends and your targeted leads. This will tell you whether those friends can make a good enough introduction for you. Now you can know the best possible path to a warm introduction.

According to Alex Devkar, CEO of Conspire:

> The problem with other professional networks is that they do not accurately reflect a person's real relationships. First, the model of sending a connection request and accepting means all connections look the same—whether you met someone for 5 minutes or worked with them closely for 5 years. Second, you have to manually maintain their list of connections by adding new ones and removing fading connections, which in practice does not happen.

A similar sentiment comes from Mark Roberge, chief revenue officer of HubSpot, who would rather have his sales reps sell to people they know instead of focusing on predetermined territories.

> If you think about territories, they grew out of sales teams who knocked on doors. That's the whole point. Put your people where the doors are. For whatever reason, it is still

around. Either way you should organize your sales team by the buyer persona.

Having a usable network is a huge advantage. Make sure it's well leveraged by your sales team and organization.

Also check out KiteDesk to see which business connections you could leverage to gain access to your Accounts in Salesforce. Connection strength is scored in order to tell you your best possible access point.

In addition, take a look at ProLeads to get a view of your best path to contact a lead and insights into what to put in the initial e-mail you send to that lead.

Getting Information on Your Individual Prospect

Discover.ly   Discover.ly has taken the place of Rapportive in my Gmail. It is a social app that works within Gmail; it sits in Gmail as a browser extension and produces information from social accounts linked to the recipient's e-mail address. Sales reps can also use Discover.ly to quickly verify e-mails within Gmail by typing in the best-guessed e-mail address and seeing if a profile comes up.

The e-mail plug-in Rapportive is still a valid option, but Rapportive hasn't done much to stay ahead of the curve since the LinkedIn acquisition.

FullContact is a platform that pulls from the social profiles of all of your contacts so that you have all of the necessary social media information handy in your CRM system. It's also great for syncing, cleaning, verifying, and de-duplicating contact lists.

For more on trigger events, and when and why to reach out, I recommend reading top blog posts from Craig Elias, Jamie Shanks, Jeff Hoffman, John Barrows, and Daniel Barber, all thought leaders on Trigger Event Selling™.

CHAPTER 7

Segmenting

The first message you send to prospective customers is absolutely crucial, so this first-touch e-mail needs to work in your favor. The only way to personalize your messaging in a scalable manner is to get really good at segmenting your lists. This allows you to hit a full list with a note that is tailored to all of them yet is still fairly general.

Here's an example of how a company called The Storefront used segmenting to properly personalize their message at scale.

The Storefront was a marketplace for pop-up shops and short-term retail rentals. When it opened in cities across the United States, The Storefront needed to market its services to both landlords and retailers, so it found websites in which the contact details for landlords (Yelp, Tripadvisor) and for retailers (Etsy, Kickstarter) were listed.

The Storefront then used Import.io to extract all contact details from the websites into neatly ordered lists, which it could export into Google Docs. When The Storefront extracted contact details, it also extracted as much additional information about the leads as possible. The Storefront used this additional information to further segment lists so that it could create message templates that generated highly personalized messages for each lead.

One way The Storefront segmented the lists was by neighborhood. When it was building the list for New York City retail spaces, The Storefront scraped space listings from Yelp. This gave it all the contact information it needed and also grouped the leads by neighborhood. By pulling this information, The Storefront could put together a personalized template geared toward companies in specific areas of New York City, like Soho or Tribeca.

The Storefront would send an e-mail to the companies with a mention of the neighborhood they were in and the other stores in that neighborhood that were already listing on The Storefront. This made the message feel a lot more personal to the store owner, but it was still a mass message sent in an e-mail campaign. For example, an e-mail would say, "We've been running pop-up shops with store owners in [neighborhood] successfully for over two years now. Your neighbors [Store1] and [Store2] are also utilizing the marketplace to rent out their spaces."

The message seems personalized, but all of the information was pulled from the CSV (comma separated values) file that The Storefront created. Nothing had to be manually filled in. This is the power of careful segmenting.

Figure 7.1   Store Fronts

WHERE TO START SEGMENTING

Once you have lists, contact information, and some research, you should have a good idea of how to segment your lists. First separate out all of the leads for which you have warm introductions. Using the tools mentioned in previous chapters, you should be able to figure out which accounts you can get introduced to. That's probably your best way in.

Next, you can take a look at where you pulled the lists. For example, if you scraped the list of companies that sponsored at Dreamforce, it is already a well-segmented list. You can use the fact that they sponsored at Dreamforce in your message. In an e-mail to this full list, you can say something like, "Companies that sponsor Dreamforce see X value with our product" or "I really enjoyed chatting with the reps in your booth at Dreamforce and I would love to continue the conversation." This gives it some personalization, but it requires that you segment your lists properly.

Again, the deeper you can segment your lists, the more personal you can get while still contacting multiple companies. If I took the Dreamforce list and then pulled out the companies on the list that perform a certain service, I have a list that's even more targeted. Hence, my messaging could emphasize that they were at Dreamforce and also performed a certain service, making the message look more personalized than before, while still hitting numerous companies.

Start playing with other reasons to segment your lists based on alerts, triggers, or how you built the lists in the first place.

I recently met with an e-commerce company out of Singapore called TradeGecko. TradeGecko was getting plenty of inbound e-mails from e-cigarette companies that wanted to use their back-end inventory management software. By using this information, TradeGecko was able to build a list of e-cigarette distributors in the United States and the United Kingdom for its first outbound messaging sales campaign. This was a well-defined list with a targeted message, and it had a high success rate for them. TradeGecko segmented on location and industry, but you can experiment.

Since this was TradeGecko's first outbound campaign, it did not have results to compare the campaign to; however, TradeGecko was blown away by the response. Over 50 percent of the e-cigarette companies TradeGecko had reached signed up for a free trial of TradeGecko.

Deeper segmentation allows you to be more targeted with your messaging, leading to fewer spam complaints and higher positive response rates. It is extremely important to make sure you're sending e-mails that will elicit a positive response. Doing this at scale is both a science and an art that can be mastered.

With new changes to their InMail policy, even LinkedIn is finally rewarding people for contacting people the right way. LinkedIn has said:

> InMail credits will be returned for every response, rather than for no response: InMail messages that get any response (Reply or Not Interested) from a recipient within 90 days will be credited back to you. If you don't get a response within 90 days, however, the InMail credit will not be replaced.

There aren't very many tools I've found that will strictly help with segmenting lists. It's a very intuitive process that is up to you to decipher. It isn't hard, but the more you can think through the possibilities and further segment your lists, the easier it will be to personalize messages at scale.

BUT WHAT ABOUT WHALES?

Here's the last point about segmenting lists for companies with a large average deal size or big partnerships.

Take the top accounts, maybe the top 10 percent or 100 accounts that you want to access and have really good information on, and e-mail them with strong, targeted e-mails. Save the mass e-mailing for the rest of your accounts. For these big deals, you want to be spot-on and authentic. Provide value, and really get them attracted from the beginning.

Sometimes, if you're lucky, your low-hanging fruit and whales will overlap. I was working with a company looking to go after companies with corporate learning and development budgets. The companies in this space were types like General Electric, Levis, and Coca-Cola, each of which spends millions per year on internal training. All I had to do was visit the competitors' websites that listed case studies and quotes. Not only did we know the company had a budget and was allocating it in this way, but by observing who the quotes came from, we also were able to get the buyer's name and title at that company.

Figure 7.2   Bagging Six Figure Deals

These leads would be in what I consider the top 10 percent.

Visit www.SalesHacker.com/library for more information on finding contact information, conducting lead research, and segmenting your lists.

CHAPTER 8

Outbound E-Mailing and Messaging

Thil is a long but incredibly important chapter.

To recap where we are at this point in the sales process:

- You have your list of target companies.
- You cleaned them for duplicates.
- You know whom you want to reach at the companies.
- You have their contact information.
- You did your research.
- You have the lists properly segmented.

Now you'll learn:

- What types of messaging are effective in getting positive responses
- A/B testing and e-mail optimization
- What metrics to measure and how to use that information to take action
- How to set up a cadence and how often and for how long you should send e-mails
- The top tools in the B2B Sales space and how to use them
- How to turn negative responses into positive responses

You're ready to start activating your prospects, but before you send anything, you need to focus on your message. There are a lot of resources available that show you how to write cold e-mails.

For subject lines, check out fun and insightful articles from Copyblogger, HubSpot, Buffer, and Quick Sprout.

For the body of the e-mail, I recommend that you check out *The Boron Letters* and Neville Medhora for AIDA copywriting help. See SalesFolk.com and BreakthroughEmail.com for help on writing cold e-mails.

Additional suggested reading in the resources appear in "Resources and Programs" at the end of this book. For now, I am going to focus on the topic of outbound e-mailing. Check out the resources suggested above for sample e-mails.

The tools used for sales automation have changed the game for those who embrace science in sales. You can track, measure, and optimize like never before. You can see when, where, and how long someone is reading your e-mail. If you have a link or a presentation, that can also be tracked. The level of visibility you can get these days is incredible. However, what really matters is what you decide to do with this information.

A/B TESTING AND OPTIMIZING E-MAILS

Before you create your campaign, it's best to understand the process. You'll want to test a few things:

- Opened or viewed rate—this is the strength of your subject line
- Click-through rate—this is the strength of your call-to-action
- Response rate—this is the strength of your message
    - For response rates, I usually only count positive or luke-warm responses. Negative responses like "take me off your list" don't count, but they should be read for feedback purposes.

The best way to optimize for each of these is to A/B or multi-variable test your e-mails and send them through one of the e-mail campaign tools so that you can get accurate metrics. The previous segmenting we did earlier was also helpful for the following reasons:

- Segmenting and results based on segmenting help you measure and optimize e-mail campaigns. Sometimes you'll just have a low-performing segment or list for one reason or another.

- It's easier to send batches of e-mails. I recommend sending 50–100 e-mails per day, per single e-mail address. When you send fewer than 50 e-mails, your sample size is too small and you're going too slowly. When you send more than 100 e-mails, you start to trigger spam filters in Gmail.

- Smaller lists allow you to personalize to your audience based on buyer persona. So, if your list is a vice president of marketing in a company that is based in Boston and is in the health care industry, you can tailor the message to that buyer persona and hit the entire list at once with a much more personalized message.

The first thing to start with is the subject line. Take a subset of your lists, at least 50–100 e-mails per test, and start sending the same e-mail, but with different subject lines. Do this four times. Then take the e-mail with the highest open rate, and use that one as the baseline in a new test with three other subject lines.

The appropriate person or introduction request subject lines from earlier in the book are my baseline e-mails to test against. These subject lines have been shared across the Internet, so I'm surprised they still work, but they still do, somehow. The goal is to get open rates at a minimum of 30 percent.

Keep testing until you get there, but don't stoop to low levels just to get high open rates. Using an artificial forward or reply is a way to trick someone, and the person will know that. If you play tricks, you'll abuse your prospects' trust before you ever get a chance to open a dialogue, and that's not going to bode well for you.

One thing to test is using the person's name or the company name in the subject lines. This makes the e-mail look more personal before the recipient even opens it.

Next, test different locations and languages for your call-to-action, using either links or attachments. Try to make sure your e-mails look like casual e-mails and not marketing e-mails when you do this.

Lastly, the body of the message should be short and to the point. Don't give too much information. Provide value for the recipients, feel their pain, talk about them—not yourself. If you have done your research and you are reaching out individually instead of mass e-mailing, then you should know what their initial problems might be.

Always go into this opening e-mail campaign with the goal of setting up the first call. Do not aim too high or ask for too much. Be strong, and lay out a certain time to speak. Don't ask.

Even though you are collecting information on open, click-through, and response rates, the only thing that you need to worry about in your pipeline is the number of meetings that you set up. You are using all of these e-mail metrics to make your e-mails better so that you can set up more meetings.

The numbers will vary by whom you ask and the type of business, but you'll want to aim for numbers like the following:

- Open rate: 30–50 percent
- Click-through rate: 20–35 percent
- Response rate: 15–30 percent
- Meeting set-up rate: 10–20 percent

There are many other variables at play here that could lead to skewed numbers. Some of these variables are the following:

- Poor performing lists
- Server or sending issues
- The sales rep who is sending the e-mails
- Time of day and/or the date

To counteract some of these variables, do research. According to the sales automation company Yesware, your e-mail has a very low chance of being opened if it hasn't been read within the first 24 hours.

Many experts advise sending e-mails at 9:00 AM local time on Tuesday and Wednesday. Some like to send e-mails from 3:00 to 6:00 PM local time on Tuesday and Wednesday to catch people as they're getting out of work. Others say that sending e-mails on weekends is best, since people don't get a lot of e-mails then, so yours will stand out more.

There are many different studies and justifications for timing e-mail campaigns. I recommend that you take advice from a few sources and see what works best for your audience. Again, you can always lean on your allies. Don't be afraid to ask what works for people in your product's space who aren't competitors. Save yourself some time.

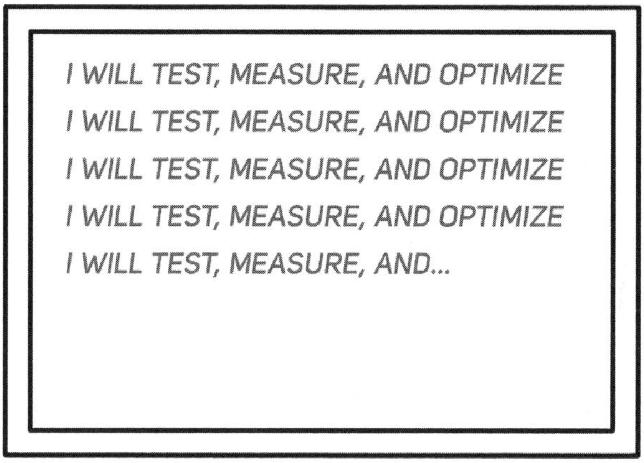

> *I WILL TEST, MEASURE, AND OPTIMIZE*
> *I WILL TEST, MEASURE, AND OPTIMIZE*
> *I WILL TEST, MEASURE, AND OPTIMIZE*
> *I WILL TEST, MEASURE, AND OPTIMIZE*
> *I WILL TEST, MEASURE, AND...*

Figure 8.1   Test, Measure, Optimize

DETERMINING YOUR PERFECT CADENCE

Outbound sales campaigns also go by cadences or sequences and are run through e-mail automation software. A cadence is considered your outbound messaging rhythm in which you mix in various types of contacting, such as through e-mail, social media, and the phone, over a set period of time. Maybe you call on day 1, e-mail on day 2, and call and e-mail on day 5. This is a sample of a cadence that you can create for contacting potential buyers.

I'll go over the tools for doing this shortly, but, first, here are some high-level strategies to understand.

When you are setting up outbound sales campaigns, you'll need to pick a number of touches per lead and decide how to contact them.

Recently, HubSpot ran a study that said that, after nine touches, you've reached the point of diminishing returns. In the advertising world, they say that customers need to see your brand seven times before they can start to recognize it.

Tawheed Kader, the chief executive officer (CEO) at ToutApp, calls his cadence the "five by five" (five contacts, or touches, over five days). Kyle Porter, the CEO of SalesLoft, calls his cadence the "seven by seven" (seven contacts, or touches, over seven days).

According to Kevin Gaither, vice president (VP) of inside sales at ZipRecruiter,

> Most outbound reps give up after one to three attempts to a lead, but statistics from www.InsideSales.com and Velocify show that you'll need six to nine touches to establish contact and qualify the lead. Once you've made your six to nine touches over a three-week period, only then should you put your lead into a Nurture Queue for follow up at a later date.

John Barrows, one of the leading sales trainers and sales development rep (SDR) trainers for Salesforce, Marketo, LinkedIn, Box, Zendesk, and others, says you should keep contacting potential customers until they give you a response or a definitive "no." Then he recommends following up again in a few months.

I tend to agree with John. I think the best salespeople are very persistent. In sales, "no" is the second-best answer. "Yes" is the first, but a "maybe" or not receiving an answer at all are by far the worst. This seems to be something nobody in sales can agree on, but I think it's something that should be different for every business. It depends on deal size, pipeline, number of leads and active leads, and other factors. This is where you can play around and see what's best for you.

Here's where segmenting comes into play again. You'll have maybe two or three groupings of leads. The top group, your whales or low-hanging fruit Fortune 500 companies, would get phone calls built into your campaign. The next group would only get e-mails, but with a high personal touch (meaning, deeply segmented, or somewhat customized). The bottom group would get a standard outbound drip campaign from the salesperson until they responded.

I don't like calling everyone, but some salespeople do. I think you need to have extra resources for that to work well. If you're an individual sales rep with a territory at a big company, go ahead and call everyone. But if you're a cofounder or an early stage sales hire, you're probably spread too thin to call every single outbound lead.

I also don't like stopping a cadence, but some salespeople do. Only when people reply do they get taken off the list. If it's a hard "no," you can reach out again in six to nine months to see if the timing is better. As the campaign goes on, time between e-mails should lengthen to a maximum of two weeks. Basically, if you're hitting the right person with the right message at the right time, you shouldn't stop until you have a hard "no." The sales industry experts have very different opinions about this, but it depends on your company, process, value proposition, and personnel. I like to call the best leads first and then send e-mails to the less important leads until I set up a warm call.

THE SERVICES THAT POWER OUTBOUND SALES

Companies offering services that power outbound sales are my favorite because of how useful they are. Each one of these companies has the potential to be a billion-dollar company and the best friend of salespeople everywhere.

Users can build and optimize e-mail templates, and A/B test, track, and send e-mails to groups of prospects all at once. Some of the companies have much deeper analytics for managers, which we won't discuss very much in this book. Many integrate with Salesforce, Gmail, Outlook, and other customer relationship management (CRM) systems, so they should be able to handle whatever systems your company is built on.

The following tools are being used across organizations, not just in sales.

Cadence (from SalesLoft)

I went over SalesLoft's prospecting and lead-generating tool in Chapter 5, but recently SalesLoft has released a new product that allows you to take those leads and start prospecting. Its tool is built directly for both the outbound and inbound SDR, and helps them not only with e-mail contacting but also with phone contacting. For example, you can set up and run a campaign inside of Cadence that consists of e-mails and phone calls that looks like this:

- Day 1: E-mail.

- Day 2: Call in the morning.

- Day 3: Call in the morning without voicemail; call in the afternoon with voicemail.

Featured Use Case Study   Insightpool has dedicated its entire outbound sales process to the Cadence tool. Cadence is the application of record for the SDR team, helping the team create, maintain, and improve on the phone call and e-mail process. The system gives the sales reps a simple process to follow for creating e-mail templates, tracking and analytics, power phone call dialing with voice recording, notes storage, and syncing with a CRM system.

Check out SalesLoft's Top Secret SDR Playbook for guidance on setting up your Cadence.

Outreach.io

Outreach.io is a really strong new player in the outbound sales space, with a solid team and a sturdy product. The key difference between Cadence and Outreach.io is that, instead of firing a pixel, like all other e-mail tracking software companies, Outreach.io hooks into your SMTP (Simple Mail Transfer Protocol) server. RelateIQ did this in the CRM space and found that this gives you better and more accurate data on your replied rates. RelateIQ is also fairly intuitive. It filters out duplicate e-mails automatically and gives you recommendations on the best times to send your e-mails and how many e-mails to send.

Featured Use Case Study   The sales team at Datanyze was looking to automate cold outbound outreach and put it on cruise control. The sales team wanted to create a series of touchpoints that would stop upon a reply from a prospective customer.

The sales team at Datanyze had two requirements:

- Reply detection had to be bulletproof. Datanyze could not afford an e-mail going out to a prospect who had already engaged with sales.

- They needed to be able to easily A/B test their e-mails and change things on the fly. The sales team was extremely metrics driven and wanted to use testing as a way to improve conversion from current leads.

Since using Outreach.io for outbound sales, Datanyze has hit 50 percent reply rates for cold e-mails—a number that previously had been impossible to achieve.

Outreach.io also serves as the midfunnel sales touchpoint for inbound teams. SDR and marketing development rep (MDR) teams have the ability to reply to inbound leads with one-to-one personalized sales e-mails coming directly from the sales rep based on lead attributes.

Outreach.io integrates with Salesforce, Outlook, and Gmail.

ToutApp

ToutApp is designed to help sales and business development professionals manage, track, and gain insights from their e-mails. Over the last three years, ToutApp has been able to develop a very robust and invaluable sales tool that is now being used across entire organizations. ToutApp built an incredible team out of San Francisco that has done an amazing job in growing sales reps who have had little previous experience. Without much funding and only one full-time developer, ToutApp has come a long, long way.

Some of the more advanced features of ToutApp are the following:

- A live feed, so users can see in real time when an e-mail recipient opens the e-mail, clicks on a link, or opens an attachment, as well as what page of the attachment the recipient has read and what page of the user's website the recipient is viewing.

- Group e-mails that can easily be searched for all those who haven't responded so that a follow-up message can be sent to them.

- Visual tracking of prospects' engagement through their views, clicks, and replies.

- Scrapes contact information from any website and ensures that ToutApp and Salesforce are always up to date.

ToutApp plugs directly into both Gmail and Outlook, and it has a deep integration with Salesforce, so sales reps and managers can access ToutApp data and tools from anywhere they like. ToutApp also integrates with marketing automation platforms like Marketo so that sales and marketing reps can stay in sync and see what messaging is resonating the best with prospects to move them through the pipeline.

Featured Use Case Studies   By tracking with ToutApp, a director of hospitality sales at an NBA franchise was able to close two six-figure deals in one month, which he wouldn't have been able to close otherwise. With the first deal, he was able to see his e-mail being forwarded to multiple people at the prospective company and that the recipients were actively engaged and interested, so he gave them time to continue gathering information, and then he followed up at the right time.

With another prospect, the director was having a hard time getting in touch with someone whom he already knew would be interested in purchasing a suite. The prospect went dark, and there was no contact for several months, until the prospect popped up on the director's live feed one day. The director called the prospect while the prospect was looking at his e-mail and closed the deal on the same call.

Yesware

Yesware is an e-mail productivity service for salespeople and is another one of the major companies in the outbound sales space. It has only been around for a few short years but has created a great product for today's salesperson. Yesware has double the head count of ToutApp and has raised four times as much money. It is based in Boston and now has offices in San Francisco as well.

Some of the more advanced features of Yesware are the following:

- Yesware Mobile allows sales reps to send and track e-mails and to access e-mail templates through their mobile device. Activity is automatically synced with Salesforce data.

- Swipe-to-call allows a sales rep to call a prospect directly from an e-mail thread. Yesware's data shows that responding to a recently opened e-mail results in a 30 percent higher connection rate. This tool allows a salesperson to quickly reach out once an e-mail event takes place, even while the sales rep is on the go.

- Yesware's presentation tracking feature gives deep insight into how engaged a prospect is with any content that is being shared. Sales teams are able to see how many people were sent the presentation, how many views the presentation received, and the average time recipients spent viewing the presentation.

Significant use yields larger amounts of collected data, which builds a more complete picture for sales reps and managers when they are analyzing individual performance, team performance, best practices, progress over time, and so forth. In addition, Yesware provides actionable insights. For example, Yesware's data shows that Monday is not the best day to send an e-mail. The highest number of opened e-mails occurs on weekends.

Featured Use Case Study Acquia took advantage of the e-mail-tracking feature in Yesware to collect data around various events, like e-mail opens, link clicks, and attachment views. This information allowed Acquia to take a great deal of the guesswork out of the sales process, resulting in fewer touches to move a deal through the pipeline.

The information also made it easier for sales reps at Acquia to prioritize prospects and determine their next steps, including when they should call.

Sales reps who called a prospect immediately after the prospect opened an e-mail, clicked a link, or opened an attachment connected with that prospect over 34 percent of the time. Overall, Acquia's use of Yesware data to determine who and when to call improved the sales reps' overall call connection rate by 29 percent.

SalesforceIQ

In 2014, Salesforce acquired RelateIQ for a whopping $390 million, but the service just released and became a lot better. SalesforceIQ integrates very well with other services you're using, without the need for an external integration tool. The best integration is via your e-mail's SMTP server, similar to Outreach.io, and of course, to Salesforce. This allows SalesforceIQ to pull in information from your e-mail and calendar and to give you a clearer look at your data for each lead.

SalesforceIQ's filtering and its Gmail extension are probably its strongest assets. It's nice when you can use a CRM tool from Gmail without having to open new tabs. The CRM filtering was built in an intuitive way that allows you to sift through data both accurately and easily.

Cirrus Insight

Cirrus Insight is a plug-in for Gmail and Outlook that automatically updates Salesforce as you work. Some of my favorite features include the ability to track e-mail opens, to share available meeting times, to merge e-mail templates, and to sync e-mails and calendar events with Salesforce. The best part about it is that it allows sales reps to stay in one screen without the need to click around and get bogged down in tedious data entry tasks.

PersistIQ

PersistIQ is an outbound sales platform—an interesting up-and-comer in the SDR space. The product is well built, with key features such as the ability to de-duplicate e-mails and to show your previous conversations with a lead from Salesforce. The product is very similar to Outreach.io and Cadence.

Pouyan Selehi, CEO of PersistIQ, says that he built PersistIQ because:

> We think reps should focus on the quality of your outbound sales instead of just quantity. This means take the time to think through and create prospect profiles and create targeted messages. Try different messages, wait different periods of time between touchpoints, and segment differently. Find what works for you.

LiveHive

LiveHive adds a bit of prediction on top of the e-mail automation process. With LiveHive, you get e-mail opens, link clicks, document downloads, page-by-page analytics, and can see the time you spend on each page of sales collateral. LiveHive then analyzes these behaviors to help prescribe the best course of action based on past results. The feature SmartPath allows you to set up e-mail sequences and add and remove leads on the fly.

Sidekick (from HubSpot)

HubSpot's Sidekick is a little different from the other Enterprise Players. HubSpot's claim to fame is that its product is made more for the sales rep than for the manager.

Brian Balfour, who leads growth for Sidekick at HubSpot, explains:

> Sales reps need tools that make their day faster, more productive, and more efficient. We developed a tool with the sales rep in mind, growing adoption through the frontline sellers, and learning what their specific needs are.

Sidekick has an activity feed for sales reps so they can be notified about actions in real time. Obviously, Sidekick has deep integrations in

HubSpot's marketing and CRM software, as well as in Salesforce. If you're already heavily reliant on HubSpot, this might be a good option for you.

A unique integration that I like is Sidekick's connection with Zapier. Sidekick syncs with the various tools and apps that are available through the Zapier app exchange. For example, sales reps can sync with Twitter and Sidekick to get customized tweet notifications in their Activity Stream, and Sidekick also syncs with Zendesk to get support case information.

SALES AND CUSTOMER SUCCESS

The following tools were built for the sales organization, more specifically, SDR teams.

Sendbloom

Sendbloom is a sales-driven sales automation platform in the SDR space. Its goal is to allow you to more deeply segment your lists and to engage with the prospects at scale. Sendbloom's system actually builds in more data about your leads for you and then helps you figure out how to segment your lists and craft messages that will create action in that specific segment.

Sendbloom helps sales and marketing development teams nurture target accounts and stay on top of inbound leads. SDR teams need to know that there is no one-size-fits-all message. With Sendbloom, SDR teams can create conditional segments for their leads based on criteria like the prospect's title and analytics stack. The product is doing this research for them programmatically, and only the prospects that don't reply receive another message.

For testing how e-mails will look on different devices and on e-mail clients' servers and browsers, check out E-mail on Acid and Litmus.

QUICK TIPS ON MESSAGING PSYCHOLOGY

Consider the following tips in order to communicate clearly and build rapport with your target customers through your outreach.

1. Pay Close Attention to the Words You Use

Think about this for a second. If we're partnering on a project, and I tell you that you're going to have a lot of responsibility, you'll see that as daunting and stressful. If I tell you that you'll have a lot of control, you'll see that as freeing, and you might be enthusiastic. They both mean the same thing, but because of the wording, each comes across differently to the other person.

There's a big difference in someone's mind when you use the word *contract* versus the word *agreement*. But often they mean the same thing.

When I left Udemy, I wrote messages to people in my personal network, asking them to introduce me to companies that needed a business development lead. I knew I wanted to stay at a small start-up, but I wanted to explore all of my options, and I didn't want to consider offers while I was still with Udemy.

One thing to know and never forget: it's not what you ask that's important; it's how you ask it. Instead of saying, "I just left my company. Do you know anyone who is hiring?" say, "I just left my company. If you know anyone looking for a skilled business development person, do them a favor and introduce them to me." It completely flips the script. Whether it is written or relayed in verbal communication, a lot can be achieved in how you phrase things.

2. Keep It Short, and Dumb It Down

Nobody wants to hear your jargon- and abbreviation-riddled, multi-paragraph sales pitch. Even worse are salespeople who use big words to sound smarter or more knowledgeable. In the end, you will lose potential customers because you're not making it easy enough on them.

Keep communication easily readable for your recipients so that they can digest the information quickly and take action. Imagine that your recipients are reading your message on their smartphone on a bus ride home after a long day at the office. You'll want to make sure that your message is short and easy to read. That's the only way they'll read it all the way through and take action.

Be sure to make the key points and preferred actions clear; you may even want to highlight them in bold.

Instead of using the word *utilize*, choose the simpler word *use*.

Don't use abbreviations unless they're universally well known in the industry, like CRM or ROI (return on investment). Acronyms such as Customer Life Time Value (CLTV), Customer Acquisition Cost (CAC), and Average Revenue Per Account (ARPA) are not used universally. Stay away from using words, phrases, and acronyms that the recipient may not understand.

Don't be afraid to go against the principles of writing in your e-mails. This isn't your high school honors English class; this is an important message to a busy potential buyer. Try adding more spacing in your e-mails—separate paragraphs every two sentences. Make it easy for readers to scan or read your e-mails quickly.

Make your message simple enough for an eight-year-old to understand.

3. Don't Be Afraid to Challenge People

When you are setting up an outbound messaging campaign or to make sales in general, you'll need to have a thick skin and sometimes a short memory. There will always be people with a poor attitude who reply to your messages. Just keep pushing, but do it the right way. You're just doing your job, and know that for every 1 person who responds negatively, you'll sign up 50 more.

Don't ignore the negative people, either. Sometimes a great way to reply is by challenging them.

At Udemy, we would sometimes get poor replies from experts. As we refined our sales process, we received fewer and fewer negative replies, but it still happened once in a while. If we read the situation well and knew a little bit about the recipients' background, sometimes we could flip them. Sometimes I would respond with a challenge. I would find two big-name experts in their space whom they knew, and I would reply in the following manner:

Hi [First name],

Sorry to have bothered you. I thought you were on the level of [expert 1] and [expert 2] who are both doing extremely well on Udemy. That's why I thought this would be perfect for you, but I guess I was mistaken.

I will make sure you do not receive another e-mail from us.

Again, I apologize.

Best,

Max

In this case, you're challenging them by saying that if they do not see the value of your service, they must not be such a big-name expert. Some people will call your bluff and not respond; others will respond with a simple "thanks." But sometimes, and more often than not, you'll get a response such as, "Oh I didn't know [expert 1] and [expert 2] were at Udemy. Maybe I will have a few minutes to chat this week."

4. Sell to the Individual, Then the Employee, Then the Company

The people on the other end of your messages are individuals, first and foremost—human beings with feelings, emotions, wants, and needs. Appeal to them as individuals first, making them feel like they'll be more special or important if they listen to you. Then appeal to their career goals, and explain how using your company's services will make them look good to their boss. Lastly, appeal to them by providing the tools they will need to sell the rest of the company on your product. For example, describe how using your services will make them look like a hero to their team and how their team will become more productive and generate more revenue—tell them how to sell your services to the key stakeholders.

Here are a few more things to note when you are conveying a message via e-mail, from cold e-mail expert and CEO of Salesfolk, Heather R. Morgan:

- Make your e-mail conversational and human. Don't write like a robot or be gimmicky like a marketer.

- Be persuasive. Try to evoke emotions.

- Talk about your product or service in terms of benefits instead of features. For example, say, "Use this process to triple your response rates" instead of "This feature helps with A/B testing to write better e-mail copy."

- It's more convincing to show the benefits of using your services in the form of a case study sentence rather than simply telling them. Use a statistic, if possible. For example, say, "Our e-mail copy helped [Client] double their qualified leads in a month, which also doubled their sales team's quota."

- Try to add value, evoke fear of loss, or play on people's competitive nature.

- Be focused, and don't try to cover too many tangential points in one e-mail.

- Develop a clear persona for each segment list.

- Introduce only one concept or idea per e-mail. If you have a lot of value propositions and ideas, relax, and save them for other touches in your campaign.

- Send six to eight e-mails for every person you're reaching out to.

- In some cases, you may actually get more responses by sending six to eight e-mails than any other touch point earlier in your campaign. Even if this isn't the case, it's still worth it to get the people who respond on e-mail six to eight that would have otherwise stayed cold.

- Test everything. Every persona and industry is different, so you need to test things to find out what works.

- Stay away from long sentences or long paragraphs.

- Don't be afraid to ask for things or demand things; just do it politely.

- The difference between being pushy and persistent is politeness.

- Try putting the company name in the subject line.

Visit www.SalesHacker.com/library for more guidance on cold outreach and outbound e-mail messaging campaigns.

CHAPTER **9**

Sales Outsourcing

If you look back through the past few chapters, you'll start to pick out many tasks that are menial and tedious. This is a why a virtual assistant (VA) becomes useful in any organization, no matter how small that organization is. You should be leveraging these inexpensive, but qualified, workers.

At Udemy, we employed a lead generation team of 12 virtual sales development reps (SDRs). They did everything from generating leads to sending batches of e-mails and setting up meetings. Eventually, they worked throughout the entire company, doing everything from website bug testing to instructor support.

I have a team of three to four VAs working at all times. They're such an asset and can do anything in the sales process. If you can nail this piece of the process, it's to your advantage as a salesperson or a sales organization.

Here are a few tasks VAs can do:

1. Use Import.io or Kimono Labs; they just need links to lists

2. Get leads by using any of the lead generation tools with the lists they've built

3. Do lead research by uploading lists into any of the tools in the lead research section

4. Segment and de-duplicate lists based on your orders.

5. Upload lists into sales automation software and even set up sequences

VAs can do tasks in almost the entire SDR process up to the actual phone call. You need to come up with an ideal customer profile (ICP) and addresses, give the VAs the links, tell the VAs how to segment the lists, and then craft the content.

PREPARING TO HIRE VIRTUAL ASSISTANTS

The first thing you'll want to do when you are getting ready to hire a VA is to draw out the current process for everything you would like to hand off to the VA. Once you draw out these tasks on paper, you'll be able to see what you can cut, if anything. Most of what you do in your business is likely busywork. This is Pareto's law at work: 20 percent of your work leads to 80 percent of your results, whether those results are in customers or revenue.

Find out what your bread and butter is—your 20 percent—and either cut or delegate the rest. If you can't get organized and draw this out for yourself, then you're probably doing something wrong to begin with.

HIRING VIRTUAL ASSISTANTS

You can hire VAs for all sorts of things. I'm going to break down the right ways to hire VAs and the right areas to hire them from (both Web services to use to hire them and where in the world you should hire from).

Upwork

Upwork is an innovative platform that connects employers with virtual freelancers. It has a fully stocked marketplace of great talent. You can find some of the best VAs there at a bargain.

The back end is robust as well. Upwork boasts having the best time-tracking and payment-tracking tools of any outsourcing site, which makes it best to use for managing overseas employees who are working alongside you. I've had my VAs logging 40–60 hours of work per week and usually working during our hours. It's very easy to build a full team on Upwork. You set the price at the beginning, and that's what you end up paying per hour.

Suggested Projects:

- Lead generation and link building
- Customer support
- Quality assurance (QA) testing engineer

TaskUs

We started using TaskUs at Udemy early on and found that they employ extremely high-quality virtual assistants who can do tasks throughout an organization. TaskUs gives you a fully managed back end and helps you hire the team. All you have to do is train and manage the team. This is a pretty good scenario if you don't want to deal with any logistical headaches like finding talent and paying through the Philippines. Services like Upwork do take a big fee (11 percent). So, for getting good talent and not having to deal with the back-end logistics, TaskUs might be worth using.

TaskUs works with big technology companies such as Udemy, Eventbrite, and AdRoll on anything from sales development to customer support. Suggested projects: everything, but TaskUs is a little pricier than Upwork: about $10 an hour more. They're good, though.

STRICTLY SALES DEVELOPMENT SUPPORT

LeadGenius

LeadGenius couples proprietary data and technology with a dedicated team of outsourced sales reps. It works with your sales development team to feed higher-quality leads into your company's existing sales funnel, no matter how you have it structured. LeadGenius's core offering is higher-quality customer data.

In addition to the outsourced SDRs, LeadGenius helps existing teams prioritize marketing qualified leads (MQLs), identifies buying signals for previously untapped audiences, or segments existing marketing lists for more intelligent targeting. It can also manage e-mail outreach for clients who do not have that element built into their sales funnel.

Predictable Revenue

Aaron Ross is the author of a book called *Predictable Revenue* that describes the process that built sales development at Salesforce in the early 2000s. He's a cofounder and partner of the new Predictable Revenue product.

Salesforce will help you fill the top of the funnel by figuring out your ICP and then finding those leads and other low-hanging fruit across the Internet. Salesforce has an internal sales team that reaches out on your behalf and activates the prospect. Once the prospect replies, the sales team introduces you.

Think of it as sales development as a service.

ConnectAndSell

ConnectAndSell allows you to easily ramp up your cold calling by doing the dialing for your team and connecting you to warm leads that want more information. Automated dialing is done by a mix of technology software and a team of outsourced reps. ConnectAndSell can do this while allowing your internal head count to stay the same. If cold calls are working for your team and you have endless leads, ConnectAndSell might be good to try out.

Fiverr

On Fiverr's website (yes, that's two "r"s?), you can hire people to do all sorts of weird and unique things for just five dollars. If you want something done quickly, or more of it, the extra charge is in five-dollar increments.

You can use Fiverr to find someone who will do small projects or build small e-mail lists for five dollars per task.

You can choose whom to hire based on reviews and whether the person can do your project. Physical location doesn't matter very much on Fiverr. Don't bother bargaining; it's only five dollars!

If you have a long process like an entire sales pipeline, you may want to try breaking it up and hiring multiple virtual assistants for it. I've found that it's best to hire for the exact thing that the person does instead of teaching the person a lot of different things. You can test this if you wish.

You can pay more and have someone do the entire process or pay less per VA and have a few VAs do parts of the process. You can also limit their hours so that you don't get charged a huge amount. However, with more VAs comes more management. Play around a bit, and figure out what works best for your process. My advice is to hire one "rock star" to begin with and train that VA on the entire process. Get the VA really good at it. Then he or she can go off and train and manage new VAs.

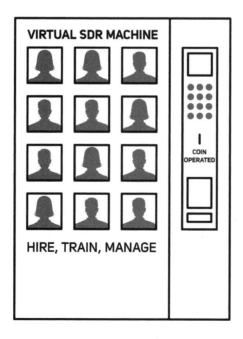

Figure 9.1 Contractor Hiring Machine

Here's a sample job posting for a lead generation task that I put on Upwork.

Title: Full-time Filipino Lead Generator/Researcher
Job Description:
About Us: Our company xxxxxxxxxxxx
Where You Fit In:
We are looking for someone to help generate leads for xxxxxxxxx

- Should be proficient in Excel and comfortable working in Google Docs

- Must have solid Internet connection 24/7—we mainly communicate via Skype and e-mail, and expect you to be online and available during the day

- Must be able to communicate in English

- Past researching or lead generation experience is a huge plus

- Must be able to work Monday through Friday, 9:00 AM to 5:00 PM Pacific Standard Time, as we are based in San Francisco

- Please send me a link to your past work.

We work with a few other tools/sites:

- Rapportive in Gmail

- Google Docs

- Salesforce

- Web scrapers and Import.io

- Twitter

- ToutApp

You should be able to pick these up quickly or have prior experience with them.

Task Example

We might ask you to find people with Twitter followings or Facebook fan pages of over 20K likes/followers. We will want them in personal finance, personal development, business, or technology verticals.

Your job will be to find these people and create a lead list with their names, community size, type of vertical, link to their company, and e-mail address. We will also have you check our database for duplicates.

Pay

We will offer between $3 and $5 per hour depending on experience and candidate selection.

If this seems like something you will be amazing at, please apply to this job post, take this brief test, and fill out the test form below.

Test:

Find the names, number of Twitter followers, and e-mail addresses for ten people on this list:
www.link.com/peoplethatareawesome

Test Form (I use Google Forms or Typeform):

Sample VA Lead Gen Test

Please write in this format for each of the 10 leads. Name, # of followers, Email address. Ex. Max Altschuler, 6134, max@blank.com

Your Name (as it appears on Upwork)

#1

Figure 9.2 Sample VA Lead Generation Test

Thanks and we look forward to working with you!

Skills Required

English, Microsoft Excel, lead generation, Internet research, data scraping, keyword research, data mining, salesforce.com, Google Docs

Notes on This Job Posting

- Some people like to give an exact direction in the description to test if the applicant actually reads the posting. For example, your description might say, "When replying to the post, please send a cover letter and make the first line read, 'I'm a rock star lead machine, and I am ready to rock!'" This is supposed to show the employer that the applicant has read the post and pays attention to detail.

- Most VAs will work during your hours.

- I start VAs at 40 hours, and then I usually increase the number of hours to 60 per week when they've earned my trust.

- I like to insert a form into the job description. It's easy to do and time-stamps their response. Make sure your first question is "Name as it appears on Upwork" so that you know who responds. I use Google Forms.

- Mention the software you use so that they know what to expect.

After about 12 hours, you'll likely have between 25 and 50 candidates. I usually pick the top few and ask them to Skype with me before I hire them. This is when I give them a timed task, which is the most important part. We know how many leads per hour is good for us, so a 20-minute sprint test is a good way to see if they can keep pace.

TRAINING YOUR VIRTUAL ASSISTANTS

When you are training your VAs, you must give them exact directions and set goals that are easy to track. This is the only way to make sure you've selected a good VA. If you hire more than one, you'll have a sample size and will know what to expect.

The best way to start is to do the task yourself and see how long it takes. If you're having the VAs do lead generation, you can set up the process and the pipeline, and do the task yourself for an hour or until you hit a certain number of leads. Time yourself, or count how many leads you've generated in an hour, and that's how many leads you should expect a good VA to generate.

For example, if it takes you an hour to collect 100 leads, then you now have a frame of reference. If it takes your VA two hours to collect 100 leads, then the VA probably is not very good. It's not unrealistic for you to expect the VA to be as good as, or even better than, you at this task, especially if the VA has done this before.

Giving the VA a task to do will also allow you to create solid directions to document the process. Take screenshots or screencasts with Jing or Skitch as you go. I like to create a step-by-step training manual that has everything the VAs need to know, as granularly as possible. This manual should have all of the logins and passwords that they'll need to know.

If the test and the manual are good and the VAs have been doing a similar job in the past, you shouldn't need to train them very much. I like to just give them the information and the task and let them get started. I encourage them to ask me questions in the beginning. The first few VAs you train will help you refine the process to the point where future VAs won't have many questions or, if they do, one of the other VAs should know the answer. That's why I advise you to get a "rock star" as the first VA.

If I have multiple VAs working for me at the same time, I can invite them to a group Skype chat or Google Group in order to answer their questions. By doing this, I might not even have to answer their questions because another VA will know the answers; or, if I do have to answer, the VAs will all know how to resolve the issue.

Make sure to have one-on-one sessions with the VAs from time to time. Matt Ellsworth, former vice president of Growth at The Storefront, likes to do an exercise called "Stop, Start, Continue" with

VAs. It goes like this: Stop doing X, start doing Y, and continue doing Z. This is a good way to give feedback to any employee, but it especially works well with VAs.

Visit www.SalesHacker.com/library for more information on hiring, training, and managing virtual assistants.

CHAPTER 10

Customer Relationship Management Software

The customer relationship management (CRM) space is crowded, and rightfully so. Jason Lemkin of SaaStr has stated that there can be multiple initial public offerings (IPOs) in this space, even for companies that fight for the bottom of the market. With one company, Salesforce, on track to do $10 billion in annual recurring revenue (ARR) soon, I believe him.

Good CRM software can be debated all day long. At the start-up level, which is the early stage to growth stage, you can use any of the ones mentioned below. They're affordable, well built, and boast an intuitive user experience.

Try to find something simple yet that is built out enough to scale with multiple deals running at the same time. If the software is too complicated and messes up your work flow, then it's not worth it.

Close.io

Close.io has a few core features as part of its CRM technology that differentiates it from other CRMs. Close.io offers voice over Internet protocol (VoIP) calling out of the box and two-way e-mail syncing, and it automatically logs all calls and e-mails to avoid any manual data entry.

Close.io also has built a search engine that enables everyone on the team to answer any questions on the fly. For example, Close.io can give you answers to the question, "Show me all leads with active opportunities that I've e-mailed longer than a week ago, that haven't responded, and for which the last call was at least seven days ago and ten minutes long." This can be a powerful feature when you are sorting through CRM data.

I recently learned that some customers actually use Close.io in conjunction with Salesforce, which enables them to get both the powerful back end of Salesforce and the user experience of Close.io.

Pipedrive

Pipedrive is known for the extreme pipeline visibility that it gives the user. The best part of Pipedrive is that it manages high-value deals and makes sure balls don't get dropped at any stage of the sales cycle. This is achieved by getting a clear picture of the sales pipeline to identify opportunities and potential issues, as well as features that encourage planning follow-ups.

Udemy was one of the first users of Pipedrive. I was drawn to the way I could get a bird's-eye view of my entire pipeline. This is very helpful for small teams with big deals.

If you're using other Web apps, you can use Zapier to connect all sorts of tools to Pipedrive and move your data automatically. For example, Pipedrive allows you to use MailChimp e-mail campaigns directly from the CRM software, using custom filters to easily create segments to send to.

Base

Base is a simple and easy-to-use CRM software. It's a turnkey solution that offers a unique suite of tools for both the sales rep and the manager.

Whether it's the initial prospecting, for which sales reps clip leads from LinkedIn into Base, or complex sales analysis, Base can do it. It's also adaptable to all industries and sales processes, from field sales to inside sales and more.

Jason Mills, head of sales at Expensify, says:

Base gives our team one central place to connect with prospects and customers, whether it's a call or an e-mail. Base also gives us a highly automated way to score and prioritize incoming prospects. Perhaps most importantly, the reporting in Base gives us immense insights into how our geographically dispersed team operates, especially in terms of the areas for improvement.

Salesforce

I foresee most companies making the switch to Salesforce at some point, even if they start with something lighter and cheaper to begin with. It's really scalable with regard to the amount of data you can store. Plus, when you hire a vice president (VP) of sales, you usually let him or her choose a CRM. Many of these potential VPs come from companies that have used Salesforce, so they already know it well. As one chief executive officer (CEO) once told me after he hired his first VP of sales, "If you hire Roger Federer, you let him choose his racket."

Salesforce's downside is that it's not made for start-ups at the moment. The price is too high, and the implementation is too difficult and time consuming to set up. It's a big investment all around.

The upside is endless scalability, both with data and hiring people who've worked in sales before. They can usually pick it up and get running full-speed immediately.

Streak is a simple CRM that is built directly into your in-box if you're looking for something more basic and easy to use.

Other CRMs that are good for large, rapidly scaling organizations include Zoho and SugarCRM.

INTEGRATION SOFTWARE

The topic of integration software isn't big enough to get its own chapter, but if you know what you're doing and can take advantage of integrations with your CRM, you can be 100 times more efficient in your sales process. These integrations let your tools talk to each other and trade information automatically.

Figure 10.1   Integration Web

Bedrock Data

Bedrock Data is an integration and data management platform that is great for your larger integrations that involve a lot of data. Unlocking the possibilities of using this data sharing between your CRM software and other tools has huge potential. For example, you can use Bedrock Data to create a custom integration, such as HubSpot to Salesforce to Recurly to Quickbooks, which is extremely powerful and will save your team a lot of time in the long run.

Also, Bedrock Data has built a great team and product, hiring some former HubSpot employees.

Zapier

Zapier, as mentioned earlier in this book, can also be used for integrations of all types—not only in your CRM but also in many stages of the sales process. You can use a simple integration like notes from Evernote that syncs to your CRM, or get a little crazier with any of the following integrations:

- Form software (Wufoo, Typeform, Google Forms)
- Support services (Asana, Zendesk)

- Chat services (Slack, Hipchat)

- Marketing automation (MailChimp, Customer.io, Vero)

- And many more

Also check out IFTTT (If This Then That) for smaller integrations like Evernote to Gmail. If you can master integration and Web-scraping solutions you'll have access to clean and actionable data across the entire Internet. This is a huge advantage over your peers.

CHAPTER 11

Nurturing Leads and Sparking Engagement

You're at the point now where you've finally started your outbound e-mail campaigns and are beginning to see responses come in. Maybe your higher-level targets haven't responded yet, but some of your e-mail campaigns are working.

At this point, you'll need to do a balance of prospecting into new leads, nurturing active accounts, and facilitating the deal for engaged potential buyers.

For prospecting into new leads, keep doing what you've been doing: build lists, segment, and test and optimize your e-mail campaigns.

For nurturing active accounts and facilitating the deal, you have a new job to do.

USING SOCIAL MEDIA TO TRIGGER BUYER ACTIVITY

Even if you haven't spoken to your leads yet, you'll want them to keep seeing your name and your company's name everywhere they go. First, make sure to surround them on social media accounts. Get out there, and engage with them on LinkedIn and Twitter. Don't use Facebook, Instagram, or more personal sites, because that will make you look too much like a stalker.

Like, share, retweet, and favorite your leads' content from time to time, allowing a few days between each post. You can even add this to your outbound e-mail campaign cadence and daily routine. This is a great task for a virtual assistant (VA). If you use a sales automation tool

Figure 11.1   Twitter Profile

with a live feed, you can have a VA do one or multiple social actions every time an action associated with that account appears on the live feed.

For example, if I see on the live feed that someone has opened my e-mail, that person should get a retweet and a like on his or her last LinkedIn comment right away. Maybe this will prompt the person to take a deeper look at the e-mail or write back. You can also use the action you see in the live feed as a reason to call the person immediately, but that goes without saying. This is more scalable, and allows you to nurture leads at scale.

You can use a tool such as Socedo, mentioned earlier in this book, to try doing this automatically.

Another thing you should be doing is sending e-mail recipients any information, news, or content that is relevant to them. You can do this on a per-prospect basis, but it can be very time consuming. Only do this for your largest accounts. You should be able to find articles that are relevant to entire list segments that you can send out.

Find triggers or action events to use as an excuse to contact leads. These triggers are the same ones mentioned earlier in this book. If the company raises money, expands, has good public relations (PR), and so on, then a congratulatory e-mail from you is in order. Make sure to take advantage of these trigger events, as they may not come around often.

A trigger event that most salespeople don't utilize is holidays. You can use any major holiday or even a Hallmark holiday as an excuse to send a warm follow-up e-mail.

Use social and lead research to see what people care most about. Maybe they are environmentalists and care deeply about Earth Day. Use that. Maybe they like to party and have a trip planned to Cabo San Lucas for Cinco de Mayo. Use that. You can also use holidays such as Halloween, Thanksgiving, Christmas, New Year's Day, Memorial Day, the Fourth of July, or Labor Day to wish someone well and follow up.

Also, if you know a person's birthday, you can wish him or her a happy birthday, and you'll be ahead of the game.

MAKE SURE TO FOLLOW UP

When you start to get responses, make sure to continue to follow up. Following up is extremely important and something that many people forget to do.

For tools to help with following up, try using Boomerang, Mix-Max, or Rebump. These tools will allow you to preset e-mails to pop back into your in-box when you're ready to reply or follow up. You can also sync an e-mail to send at a later date. Some of the outbound sales automation tools provide you with e-mail plug-ins that do similar things. MixMax allows for some basic tracking and templating, too, but it isn't as robust as Cadence or ToutApp.

I can't name names, but a successful founder friend would use Boomerang to trigger e-mails to send to investors at 3:00 AM so that it would seem as if he was working very late.

If I tell someone by e-mail that I will ping him or her in a month, it's much easier for me to get that e-mail redelivered 30 days later than to create a calendar note for myself.

REACTIVATING LEADS

With regard to nurturing existing leads, there's one tool that I like for reactivating leads that have slipped through the cracks or aren't getting the attention they deserve for one reason or another: Datahug.

Datahug

Datahug adds value throughout the sales process by

1. Helping to identify high-value leads that aren't being pursued

2. Coaching the sales team with a predictive sales coach who delivers the most effective next step for each of the deals in the sales team's pipeline

3. Enabling account managers and customer success managers to stay engaged with their customers after the initial deal closes

Datahug first identifies the key drivers of your historical deals to pinpoint the magic formula for success so that Datahug can give these insights to the sales reps. Then the sales reps can use Datahug in their weekly deal reviews to generate awareness and make it part of the sales process. Datahug creates a lot of data that makes it easier to track return on investment (ROI) and highlight stale leads or a pipeline that can be rekindled.

Datahug can surface the accounts that need action. It's up to you to take that action and make it count.

For sales reps who want to follow up while they are on the go, they can check out Immediately App and Spiro Technologies.

CHAPTER 12

Preparing for and Holding Your First Sales Call

W hen you're planning your first sales call, you'll need to become less reliant on technology and trust more in yourself, your ability to sell, and your passion. This is when it helps to have experience.

For companies with large-sized deals, the first call you make is usually your discovery call. Companies with smaller-sized deals can get right into the details.

For example, if you're selling learning and development course-ware to an executive at General Electric, and it's going to cost the company $500,000, you're probably looking at a long sales cycle with many decision makers. In this case, your first call should be about finding out a few key things. Ask questions, listen, take notes, diagnose, and then come back to prescribe.

The following are some questions to keep in mind:

- Are you in touch with the right people or key decision makers? If not, how will you get through to them?

- Do they have a budget?

- How many people will use your product?

- What are they currently using, how was it purchased, and how long have they had it?

- What are the problems with the current software or process?

- What is the purchasing process like? Is there a request for proposal (RFP)?

- How long do these types of decisions usually take?

- How many people are involved in the decision-making process, and who needs to sign off on the purchase?

- What are their problems, and how do they think you can help them? The problems may not be what you assume, and they may not fully understand what you do.

This topic alone can fill a book, so for more help with this topic, check out *SPIN Selling* by Neil Rackham, *RSVPselling* by Tony Hughes, and Jill Konrath's books.

Again, the goal is to set up another meeting with the right people. Set a time for that meeting while on the call. You don't want to pitch too much on this call, because you might not know what problem you're trying to solve yet.

If your deal size is small and your sales cycle is short, there's no need for the first discovery call. You can get right into a demonstration or larger sell immediately.

GETTING AND STAYING PREPARED

There are many smaller apps that provide nice dossiers, which are sent to the sales rep's in-box or phone before a meeting. Some even go a bit further in telling you exactly how the prospect likes to interact with other people.

Crystal

Crystal helps you communicate with others based on their unique personality, which is particularly helpful for sales reps who frequently build relationships with people they don't already know. Specifically, Crystal can contribute to the sales process by doing the following:

- Providing an accurate personality profile for any prospect, including the best ways to e-mail or speak to that prospect

- Working like spell-check in Gmail to make suggestions and improvements to the e-mail in real time.

- Giving sales reps personalized e-mail templates for common scenarios to increase the likelihood of more productive, positive responses

- Helping sales managers match prospects and customers with sales reps who have a similar communication style

For mobile and on-the-go options, check out Refresh.io and Charlie App. Both of these apps give you fantastic prospect summaries to review before you speak to the prospect.

The information you might want to know about your prospects includes the following:

- Location

- Previous job history

- College or hometown

- Social media news

- Company information or recent news about the company

- Competitors' information or recent news about the competitors

- Their social links and the events they attend

- Their recent posts on their blog, LinkedIn, and so on

- Previous conversations

Maybe you share a common interest or know the same people from a previous or current job or location. Explore anything you can uncover that you can use to bond or facilitate a meeting with them. Again, don't be a stalker! Keep very personal details and accounts like Facebook and Instagram out of it. They don't need to know you saw the picture of them and their significant other frolicking on the beach in Aruba.

Charlie App

Charlie App pulls information from hundreds of thousands of public sources to create a one-pager on all you'll need to know about someone. One of its most important features is that your one-pager can be personalized by connecting your social networks. Once added, Charlie App will tell you all the things your prospect and you share in common, whether it's people, sports teams, or hobbies. Each social media account that you connect to makes your one-pagers more personal and helps you be more effective at building rapport. In fact, Chief Executive Officer (CEO) Aaron Frazin believes that Charlie App saves an average of 57 Google searches per prospect.

Try using LinkedIn Premium with Charlie App. Charlie App automatically finds the person's LinkedIn profile and links to it in your pre-meeting research. Using the link to the person's LinkedIn profile, you can find additional background information after you use Charlie App to dive deep into the articles the person has been reading, the things he or she likes to talk about, and the breaking news about his or her company and its competitors.

Refresh.io

Refresh.io is most helpful for when you have the first or second conversation with a prospective or existing customer. The app creates a comprehensive online profile of the people you're meeting or calling, which prepares you to get the most from every conversation.

Just connect your calendar to Refresh.io, and the app will automatically research the people you're meeting. Refresh.io will even send you a push notification a few minutes before your meeting, reminding you to prepare; a full set of insights is then just one tap away. You can even set it to Auto Hide meetings with coworkers, so you're only shown external events.

Refresh.io is also a powerful tool for maintaining relationships with high-touch and high-value prospects. As you get to know a lead or customer, Refresh.io ensures that you always have a reason to reach out to that lead or customer and will never forget important details.

Before you make a call, always make sure you're prepared and know whom you're speaking to.

Once you're prepared, it's time to get on the phone with potential buyers.

PROPERLY QUALIFYING THE PROSPECT

There are many questions you might have to ask in order to properly qualify your prospects. To dramatically increase your chances of closing a deal during the first call, you will want to tap into the power of the past and the future. Here's how.

The Past

Ask your prospects about past experiences they have had buying similar products or services, and learn everything you can about their buying and decision-making process. This is particularly useful for uncovering organizational biases for or against your type of product. If you're selling software as a service (SaaS) software and they bought something in that space three months ago and are very happy with it, your chances of getting a deal done will be significantly higher than if you're the first SaaS vendor they have talked to or if their last purchase of this type was a disaster.

Following are some questions that you can ask:

- "When was the last time you bought something similar to our solution?"
- "What was that experience like?"
- "How long did it take?"
- "How many people were involved in the decision-making process?"
- "Was the purchase of that product ultimately a success?"
- "If so, why?" "If not, why not?"

The Future

Once you've learned from the past, you'll want to focus on the future. This is what I call the "virtual close." Ask the question, "What would it take for you to become a customer of ours?" Then you should stop talking and just listen. Follow up on each answer, and dig deeper until you arrive at a virtual close: "So, if we did X, Y, and Z, you would instantly buy—right?"

This process will educate you on the expected buying process, as well as show you if there is a real intention to buy, and if there are any red flags or pitfalls you should be aware of *before* you start the sales process.

Following are some questions from Steli Efti, CEO of Close.io, that you can ask:

- "What will it take for you to become a customer?"

- "Once we've done XYZ, what happens next?"

- "Are we already in business, or is there anything else that needs to happen?"

SCRIPTING CALLS

One thing in the past that's been hard to measure is how effective your call scripts are and the variations in how sales reps deliver their scripts. I'm a big fan of creating a script for calls, but I will also allow sales reps to freely go off script when needed.

Scripts also make it easy to train new hires, which gives you a faster route to positive return on investment (ROI) and on new sales development reps (SDRs), but that's not the only reason I like them. I also like them because scripts are something I can track, optimize, and measure. The main variables are the people on both sides of the phone.

Previously, you could only track whether a script was good or bad. The sales rep was either good or bad as well. With the new technological era in sales, you can now track the entire script, as well as where people tend to fall off.

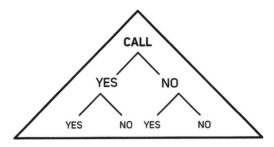

Figure 12.1   Call Tree

When you do make a call, take good notes and follow up immediately with a nice, neat, sharable version of your notes. Schedule the next call while you are on the phone. Follow up with an invite to that call, and add a reminder in the summary e-mail. Also, make sure to end with action items. For example, "Here's the information I need from you by the end of this week, before our next call . . . Here's what I will have for you by tomorrow . . . As I mentioned earlier, organization is one of the best assets that a salesperson can have. As your company grows, you'll need a better call system."

InsideSales

InsideSales provides you with a suite of tools for what they call "sales acceleration." This applies to phone calls, voicemail, Short Message Service (SMS), or "text message", e-mail, fax, and more. I like them most for the features on their call products.

Coupled with your CRM software, their platform allows you to prioritize lists of people to call based on predictive analytics and to quickly dial inbound leads as soon as they come in. According to InsideSales, "A lead called within five minutes of requesting information is over ten times more likely to answer and four times more likely to qualify."

InsideSales also allows one-click, prerecorded voice messaging and the ability to call leads from a customized local phone number, which results in increased contact rates. The new mobile app allows you to call, record, and track while you are on the go.

InsideSales also crosses over into a few other product categories, such as e-mail tracking, predictive lead scoring, and sales rep management.

SalesLoft has a new sales dialer product. I assume many of the sales e-mail automation companies will be players in this area shortly.

FORGET PINS AND ACCESS CODES

I hate personal identification numbers (PINs) and access codes, so I recommend using Speakeasy and UberConference.

Speakeasy

Speakeasy is a mobile-first platform that enables you to make conference calls, manage meetings, share presentations and screens, take notes, and sync everything to Salesforce—all from one place.

It doesn't require PINs and can even call you at the start of your call or when the first person joins the call. Speakeasy also automatically sends detailed meeting notes and log calls to Salesforce.

UberConference also works well for easy, painless conference calling.

Figure 12.2　Calendar Invite

Quick Tips in Sales Psychology

Now that you're getting on the phone, let's get you prepared psychologically. I wanted to share some interesting advice for making successful sales calls that are outside the norm.

The following is an excerpt from an article by my friend, Vanessa Van Edwards, who runs a behavior research lab and focuses on helping salespeople navigate behavioral cues. She calls it "science of people."

1. Start with a Bang

Always start with a bang. One study tried to figure out how to increase room service tips for waiters in hotels. They found there was a super easy thing waiters could do to increase their tips. All they had to do was start with a positive comment. When hotel guests opened their door, waiters said "good morning" and gave a positive weather forecast for the day. Just that one positive comment increased their tips by 27%!

How does this help you? Never start a sales meeting or pitch by talking about bad weather, traffic, or being busy. Always begin with a positive comment or anecdote. Great weather, fun weekend plans, or a favorite sports team winning a game. That gets you off onto the right foot.

2. Don't Self-Sabotage

The biggest self-sabotage mistake is to speak ill of a competitor. Research has found something called Spontaneous Trait Transference. They found that whenever you say bad things about someone else people can't help but put those same traits on you. The brain can't help but associate your gossip with you, even if logically we know you are talking about another person. If you say your competitor is low quality and unreliable, your potential client can't help but associate those traits with you. No matter what, when it comes to gossip, always say "no comment."

3. Use Awesome Labels

When you assign someone a positive label, like having high intelligence or being a good person, that actually cues them up to live up to that label. In one study about fundraising, the researchers told average donors that they were in fact among the highest donors. Can you guess what happened? Those donors then *did in fact* donate above average. We live up to our positive labels. When you are with a client or potential customer, give them genuinely good labels—I never want you to be fake or manipulative. So be sure to stick to positive truths. You can say, "You are one of our best customers" or "You're such a pleasure to do business with." In that way, they will actually want to be one of your best customers and try even harder to be a pleasure to do business with.

* * *

Now here are a few more from me:

SET THE AGENDA AND STAY IN CONTROL

When I get on a call that I set up, I always articulate an agenda for the call and then ask him or her if it is okay with them. This way, we can keep the call on track and accomplish what I want to accomplish, while at the same time making them feel in control of the conversation.

For example, "Well, I'm glad we're able to connect today. I'd love to go over XYZ and then would be happy to answer any questions you might have. How does that sound to you?"

LET THE PASSION OUT

One thing to focus on is allowing your passion and excitement about the product to show in your pitch. Make it something they can be infected by. Reps should stand up and do calls in the main room of the office. As the CEO of Mattermark Danielle Morrill calls it, "Speak loud and proud!" I myself like to pace around for all calls.

Also put an emphasis on inflection, especially on voice-mails. John Marcus, CEO of Bedrock Data, describes this as putting make-up on your calls. By adding inflection to the right words, you sound more passionate and articulate and, in turn, more convincing.

CHAPTER 13

Navigating the Buying Process and Closing the Deal

There are many steps and actions that go into closing a deal. So, congratulations on getting this far, but the reality is you're just getting started.

There's a lot of information out there on the strategy of navigating the buying process, which over the years hasn't changed all that much. Buying and procurement processes are still relatively similar year after year at the large, dinosaur-like corporations.

Before we get into the tools you'll need to better close deals, let's dive into some of the strategies from two people who are all-stars in this process and have worked on very important deals in the past. I'll tell you about more resources on this topic in Chapter 16.

John Barrows, leading sales trainer for some of the top business-to-business (B2B), software as a service (SaaS) companies, provides us with top strategies on the rules of negotiating, how to create equality in negotiations, and why you shouldn't jump to discounting.

RULES OF NEGOTIATING

1. *Rule of Reciprocity:* People have a natural inclination to repay debts.

2. *Conditioning:* Nothing comes free. Make sure to give and get.

3. *Know what to ask and when.*

4. *Follow good protocols for pre- and postconversations:* Nail down a time prior to conversations, and make sure all decision makers are able to join. Be sure to send summaries to follow.

5. *Objective health measurement:* Stay aware of the health of your accounts so that you know which ones need nurturing and which ones are ready to close.

6. *Time management:* Know what accounts to focus on first.

7. *Common language:* Make sure you relate conversation to what you are working with.

8. *Story time:* Know what stories to share and when it is appropriate to share them.

9. *Know when to walk away:* Know when a deal has died and to walk away.

True negotiations are all about coming to a mutual agreement on something, in which both parties feel like they are getting something out of the deal. Contrary to popular belief, you don't "win" a negotiation by making the other person lose. Both parties need to give and get along the way. The more equal those "gives and gets" are, the healthier the relationship is and can become.

The problem in sales is that salespeople tend to be "givers." They give and give and give, and expect one very large prize in the end as their "get" (i.e., a signed contract), and they think they've earned the signed contract because they did everything the other party asked for. However, if salespeople give throughout the process without getting much in return, they condition the client to treat them like a doormat. The client ends up having little respect for them toward the end of the negotiation process, which is why clients either keep asking for things (discounts) or just disappear and don't even have the courtesy to call back. Salespeople need to find a way to create equality in negotiations from the beginning of the relationship.

Creating Equality in Negotiations

To create equality in negotiations, most salespeople focus on a quid pro quo approach to get things in return for giving something away, which is necessary sometimes but tends to lead to a more contentious relationship. There is another approach that can be even more powerful, which is the "Rule of Reciprocity." This rule effectively states that we (as humans) are all bound, even driven, to repay debts. We don't like owing anyone anything.

If someone asks us for something, that person actually feels obligated to give us something in return. The sooner we ask for something in return, the easier it is for us to get. By understanding all the "gives and gets" along the way and matching them up, we can know exactly what and when to be asking in order to move the deal through the pipeline to closure or to get out before it's too late.

DON'T JUMP TO DISCOUNTING

- Often, salespeople jump to discounting to speed up negotiations. Discounting has such a negative impact in so many ways that it's worth pointing out a few things about it in order to gain some perspective.

- The average S&P 1000 company would suffer a 12.8 percent drop in profitability by giving a mere 1 percent discount, assuming no increase in volume.

- Salespeople make price a more important issue than buyers do (salespeople 8.3 vs. buyers 6.9).

- Whoever feels the most pressure will make the most concessions.

- Discounts kill credibility and create a negative perception of you and your solution.

- Discounts set the stage for future discounts.

So, what's the best way to combat discounting? There are some negotiation and objection-handling techniques that can help, but the best one I've come across is quite simple: just have a big pipeline. The more legitimate, healthy deals we have in our pipeline, the less desperate we are to close deals and the more confident we are in handling people who are trying to push us into discounting. We can also work more along the lines of the client's buying cycle than our

Figure 13.1   No Discounts

selling cycle. Too often, we try to force a client into our buying cycle, which typically is driven by the end of the month or the quarter. We all know sales should be about the client and not about us, so we need to do what we can to get the client to buy when he or she is ready to buy, not when we're ready to sell.

This is why prospecting on a regular basis, even at the end of a month or quarter, is so critical. Spend 30 minutes a day prospecting in some way. It can be making cold calls, sending direct e-mails, searching through LinkedIn, asking for referrals, or something else; just do it. If you're tired of using discounts to close all your deals, then prospect every day to have a consistently full pipeline and see what happens to your confidence and abilities to deal with discounting.

HANDLING OBJECTIONS

The best sales reps have gone through every possible objection ahead of time and have already planned their answers. That's why they never get caught when a client counters with an objection during negotiations.

Matt Cameron was the global head of corporate sales at Yammer before and after the multibillion dollar acquisition of Yammer by Microsoft. Before moving to Yammer, he worked his way up closing big deals when he was managing Asia/Pacific territories for Salesforce.

Matt compares the objection process to jiu-jitsu, a form of martial arts, and more specifically, to an "arm bar," which is when someone has your arm locked around theirs and it's extremely difficult to escape. When Matt was asked how one breaks an "arm bar," his reply was simply, "Don't get in that position in the first place."

The deal cycle is the same way. If you start by aligning your goals with your client's goals, you won't get stuck with common objections or roadblocks. Set common goals and timelines from the beginning, and do the best you can to hold your champion or lead buyer accountable.

After working 20 years in sales, Matt has found that the most common objections given by clients are caused by only two things:

1. You haven't sold value (to the individual, not the company).

2. Funds are not forthcoming because you haven't sold to the person with the ability to reallocate budgets.

When Matt is reviewing an opportunity with a senior sales professional, he looks for the following key elements:

-   Access to, and credibility with, executives who have the ability to reallocate budgets

-   A business case that describes quantifiable, time-bound return on investment, with an emphasis on solutions that differentiate your company from the competition

-   An articulation of how the solution will contribute to the decision maker's personal agenda

To sum up, the best way to address objections is not to receive them in the first place, but if you do, be forearmed with the antidote.

Matt also suggests using a "push counter," which tracks how many times and for how long the customer has postponed the deal. Stalling deals is the death of long-cycle sales.

DEMOS, PROPOSALS, AND COLLATERAL

Demo and presentation software is a hot area of development right now, and I, for one, am glad to see it. I don't like demo tools that make you download something, and I won't list them in this book. It's 2016—get it together.

A great demo is more than just what you put together. The software behind the demo gives customers a good user experience that they will remember and appreciate.

Whether you want to increase opportunities to sell and up-sell, improve a customer's user experience, or just engage with online customers on a regular basis, a good demo solution can increase both your chances of success and customer satisfaction.

On a basic level, there are a few things to remember when you are presenting a demo.

- Create a demo that is short and to the point.
- Don't make customers do too much to get started, and be considerate of their time.
- Go slowly, and don't talk too much.
- Ask questions such as, "What are your thoughts on this?," "Does this make sense to you?," and "Does this interest you?"
- Take good notes on customers' comments and feedback.
- Always look for ways to get better.

Most salespeople still tend to use GoToMeeting or Join.me, but here are a few other websites that I like, namely, Blue Jeans Network, Glance, ClearSlide, TinderBox, and DocSend.

Blue Jeans Network

Blue Jeans Network delivers one of the best experiences and usability of Web conferencing apps, but it's the integrations that I like most. They work well with both Windows and Mac, have a no-download plug-in within Chrome, integrate with all major calendar apps, and, best of all for me, they integrate with Slack. Blue Jeans Network also adds mobile apps for both major platforms, Android and iOS.

Glance

Glance's Panorama provides a real-time, interactive view of content, regardless of where that content resides. Glance's extremely lightweight solution allows you to present your demo within a browser, in the cloud, on a desktop, or on a mobile device. It's the best demo software that I've seen for getting a mobile demo. Best of all, you don't need to download anything to see it.

You can use Glance's Panorama to share screens, co-browse, showcase a mobile app, see the other person, or seamlessly capture data.

Glance Panorama integrates with Salesforce, Genesys, LiveOps, Oracle, Zendesk, and others to provide co-browsing, screen sharing, and agent video, as well as to capture session data for dashboards and analysis. It also provides a personal use, Server Message Block (SMB) option called Glance Lite if you don't need the Enterprise version.

Also check out Zoom.

ClearSlide

ClearSlide labels itself as a sales engagement platform that allows sales reps to get insights on how customers engage with their content by e-mail, phone, and in person.

While ClearSlide does e-mail tracking, screen sharing, and content management, the main feature I like is its presentations and proposals tracking product. Sales reps can get a good idea about what content is being digested, when, and by whom. Having this kind of visibility allows sales reps to test and optimize the content they share with customers as well as to reach out when the time is right, in the right context.

The sales rep can follow up with context and knows what points to hit on based on where the customers spend their time within the content.

ClearSlide integrates with many of the top customer relationship management (CRM) systems, content management systems (CMSs), and e-mail services.

TinderBox

TinderBox is a cloud document manager for all sales collateral and aims to be your one-stop shop from prospect, to proposal, to contract.

TinderBox integrates your CRM system with your sales collateral to allow you to create and customize proposals, presentations, or contracts based on internally approved assets. Then you can pass them along to potential customers and track and optimize the content as you go.

TinderBox tracks engagement on the content and notifies sales reps in real time when actions are taken on the customer's side. It also provides an e-signature solution for contracts that are sent through TinderBox.

DocSend

DocSend is the "new kid on the block." It allows you to do similar things like track and optimize documents on the go and get information on what happens to the document once it's in the customer's hands.

I really like their integration with Google, which is actually powered by Streak. It allows you to add content directly from an e-mail, without adding an attachment. This not only makes it easy, but it also makes sure your that e-mail doesn't backfire with a file attachment that's too big or flagged by spam. You can control the links to the content that you hand out and adjust who gets to see what.

For creating better proposals and tracking them, try using Quosal, and Qvidian.

For sales collateral, you can use either Google Drive, Dropbox, or Box. Google Drive is good to use at first, but as you get more users, you'll likely need to upgrade to something better, built to be a CMS. There's also SpringCM if you're looking for a place to put closed contracts.

You'll have to pay for these services, but if you have a lot of content and too many closed contracts to keep track of, you have what's called "champagne problems."

E-SIGNATURE SOLUTIONS

Wonderful—you've closed the deal! Now let's get the customer to sign the contract quickly.

A few good integration tools to look for are e-mail client and CRM. These make it easy to get things signed quickly. I use Google Docs integrations with contracts all the time, and they save so much time. Make sure the one you chose is also extremely secure.

Here are a few e-signature companies that work well.

- PandaDoc: Has very accurate tracking capabilities

- Nitro PDF: Has just developed a new e-signature solution

- Adobe eSign: Has robust offerings with mobile, run by Adobe

- DocuSign: Works on any device and integrates well with Google Drive

- HelloSign: Provides a good online user experience

CHAPTER 14

Business Development

In this chapter, I'll go into detail about the basics for business development and connecting with people. Interacting with people is obviously a huge part of sales, and a major key to success in the long term is building strong and lasting relationships. Here are a few of my favorite tactics and strategies for doing just that.

THE ART OF THE INTRODUCTION

A great business-to-business (B2B) introduction is an art as well as proper etiquette. It's simple. Just follow the rules below that I have put together with Outro's chief executive officer (CEO) Bubba Page, and make no excuses!

1. Who Responds First, And How Fast?

When you are making an introduction, the person who asked to be introduced (the "requestor") or the more junior person should respond first. I find that about 98 percent of the time, the "requestor" is also the more junior person.

The "requestor" should respond within one business day of the introduction being made. There should be no excuses. If you are the one who made the request for the introduction, you should respond promptly, thoughtfully, and politely once you get the introduction.

2. Double Opt-in Introductions Only

Cold, blind introductions are awful. Introductions must require both sides to opt-in. The only exception to this would be a no-brainer that everyone would respond to—for example, "Bill Gates wants to invest in/buy your company . . ."

It's a huge problem when someone makes an introduction to you and doesn't get your approval first. Now that person has put the burden on you to either respond or look like a jerk.

If someone asks you to make an introduction, reply with, "Sure. Can you send me some context I can forward along? I'd be happy to make the introduction if the person is interested in chatting with you."

Then send that along, and give an endorsement of your own if you'd like. Once the person says, "Sure. Please make the introduction." you can connect the two individuals.

3. Don't Flake Out

Once a double opt-in status has been made and both parties agree to the introduction, the responsibility lies with the requestor to respond promptly. It makes the connector look bad if the ball is dropped after the introduction has been made.

If you're too busy to follow these guidelines, don't opt-in. It will save everyone's time.

4. Move the Connector to Bcc Status

After the first reply on either side has been made, it is up to the people who were introduced to move the connector, or the person who made the introduction, to blind carbon copy (Bcc) status immediately, unless for some reason you want that person to stay involved in the conversation.

Example:

Thanks for the introduction, Bubba! (Bcc'd)
    Hey [name], it was nice to meet . . .

5. Context

As I mentioned in number 2, if you want an introduction, you must provide the connector with some context or information that he or she can forward or pass along.

Example:

Hey Max,

I see you know [name], and if possible, I'd love an introduction so that I can ask [him/her] how [he/she] navigates the process around [challenge] and potentially use [his/her] services. Is there any chance you can do this for me? Here's something you can send [his/her] way.

My good friend [requestor] is working on X and is interested in connecting with you regarding [challenge] and your company's services. Would you be open to connecting with me and providing and introduction?

Then, if I were to forward this, I would add my endorsement at the end:

I think the connection would be mutually beneficial. [He/she] is really dialed-in . . .

Note: I like the term *dialed-in* because of what it implies: it could be interpreted that the requester is both intelligent and connected.

6. Make Introductions Mutually Beneficial

This is important! Try to make introductions only when you truly believe there's real mutual benefit, even if that benefit on one side is in the future.

A subject matter expert in product management could be beneficial to [salesperson] down the line should that salesperson decide to start his or her own company one day. If you know that [salesperson] has expressed interest in being a founder, then it could be mutually beneficial later on.

- If I introduce a potential investor to a company, I better believe that that company is going to do well and that the potential investor is a person of high integrity.

- If I introduce a potential sales hire to a company, I better believe in both the potential sales hire and the company.

- If I introduce a potential client to a company, I better believe the company can produce!

7. Close the Loop

A good connector will circle back later and see if the parties have connected: "How did it go?" If the parties never connected, be sure to ask why. You may not want to vouch for that person again if he or she made you look bad by standing someone up.

8. Say "Thanks!"

As the requestor, thank the connector. Help the connector close the loop and report back to them what happened with the connection. If the introduction went *very* well, send a gift or some type of thank-you.

Sometimes when I get a gift for something I've done that makes me feel appreciated, I keep that person and his or her company at the top of my list for a while. This means that I start looking out for the person and I talk about him or her to others. Sometimes I do this without realizing it. For the business I'm in, this can prove to be very important for the person or company that thanked me.

Example: You received an introduction to an investor, and then the investor invested in your next round of funding. Or, you received an introduction to a potential client, and the potential client just signed the deal. You should send a gift basket or something even better.

9. Be Thoughtful, and Customize the Introductory E-mail

The best connectors and the most connected people I know write very thoughtful introductions. It's not just a task on their to-do list.

Being thoughtful in an introduction starts a new relationship off in the right way. Often, both parties end up talking about how awesome you are when they first connect for a conversation. You win, and they win!

Add some nice context about the people and the scenario. But don't write a novel.

Here is an example from my friend, Adam Liebman, of an introduction he sent me.

Chris, meet Max. Max, meet Chris.

Chris is currently an Associate Vice President at Mimeo, where, among other things, he helps his team to use sales tools to absolutely crush it. Chris and I worked together at Yext, and he's the first guy I would try to hire if I needed a sales leader.

Max is a man of many talents, including throwing the Sales Hacker Conferences all over the country. He also just published his first book, *Hacking Sales*, and is the man behind the idea of a "Sales Stack."

The two of you know more about sales and the tools that make sales easier than just about any other people I know. I think you'll both enjoy connecting, and I hope you get a chance to do so soon. I know Max is going to be in town next week for the next conference. Maybe all of us can find a way to get together.

I will let you two take it from there.

Cheers!

This is a great introduction. It made me excited to meet Chris, flattered me, which naturally makes me like Adam even more, and gives good context. It's too long, but in this particular case, it worked.

I think for this point more than any other, you need to "read the room." For example, for introductions to investors, it's probably best to keep them very short because their in-boxes are busier than most.

10. Provide Value

Once you've been introduced and you're looking to connect with the person, provide value, even if it's only a free lunch or drinks. If you do any research beforehand, you'll be able to provide more value because you'll know what resonates with the person.

Here is an example. Perhaps you meet with someone who is more senior than you in your profession. Professionally, you fear that there's nothing of value you can offer, and maybe you're right. But, when you do some research on Twitter, LinkedIn, and Google, you find out that the person flies planes as a hobby, and you have some background in that.

Now you can provide value when you meet, which will strengthen the relationship and ultimately make the connector look good.

Lastly, if the prospect whom you want to meet is busy, be understanding. Offer to contact the person at a better time if necessary.

If you do get introduced to someone, and you are too busy to meet the person but don't feel comfortable saying no, just tell the truth. Here is an example:

Hey [name],
        Thanks for getting in touch. I'm swamped with [task] right now and am really behind in my work. Can you ping me again in two weeks, and we can get something arranged when I know where I'm at? Thanks for understanding,

Nobody can be mad at that, and it puts the ball back in his or her court to follow up in two weeks. Also, it's very polite. And it helps you know who *really* wants to connect with you, because quite a few people will forget to follow up.

Follow these rules of introduction etiquette, and you'll be in good standing with your peers in the industry. After all, being a connector starts with being able to connect people properly. Just go the extra mile, and reap all the benefits. Your network will thank you.

ASKING FOR REFERRALS

The best time to ask for a referral is right after the deal closes. This is a "honeymoon" phase, when both parties have entered into a new and exciting partnership, yet so many people forget this step.

When you are asking for a referral—or anything, for that matter—be aware of the language you're using. Too often, I see people asking for favors in a manner that presents it as, well . . . asking for favors.

Know How to Sell It

We now come back to the phrasing we discussed earlier in this book. Consider the following request:

Hey Stan,

I'm about to start applying for jobs. Do you think there's a position open for me at your company?

as opposed to this request:

Hey Stan,

I'm fielding offers and have some great opportunities lined up, but I'd love to find a way to work with you. Are there any openings we should discuss?

Which phrasing do you think will work more in your favor? Clearly, the second one makes you look better and will leave a lasting impression on the recipient.

CHAPTER 15

Bonus Sales Hacks

I would like to share a few bonus sales hacks for you to consider building into your sales process.

E-MAIL SIGNATURE

For starters, too many people throw a bunch of images into their e-mail signatures. I don't care if it looks pretty—don't do it. Make your signature as simple as possible. The only thing you should add is a link to recent positive public relations (PR). If the title of the story isn't very good but the article is awesome, change the title in the link that you are sharing.

Example Signature

[Name] | [Twitter Handle]
[Title], [Company name]
[Mobile/Skype] | [Office/Skype]
Forbes Names [Company Name] Top 10 Fastest Growing in 2016, Find Out Why!

Just link to the Forbes article in that example signature, even if it's just a slide in the Forbes article titled "Top 10 Fastest Growing Companies of 2016."

If you're selling home owners on listing their places as short-term rentals on Airbnb, you can take an article titled, "Airbnb Raises $100 Million to Challenger Hotels," and link it in your signature with the words "Airbnb Raises $100 Million from Top Investors to Make Home Owners More Money."

My friend, Scott Britton, does this with his blog to increase traffic to his blog.

Scott explains:

> Instead of just linking my signature link to my blog, I link to each post individually following the precursor, "Most Recent Thoughts." This not only ensures my link appears since it's a new and unseen link, but also provides more compelling copy that's likely to inspire a click.

What's the Return on Investment (ROI) on This?

> It took me 20 seconds to change the hyperlink in my e-mail signature within my Gmail settings. To measure the amount of traffic this drove, I used a Bit.ly link, which I reserved entirely for the hyperlink within the e-mail signature.
>
> It turns out that *45 people* clicked on my "Most Recent Thoughts" link over the past 3 days. From those 45 clicks three people re-shared this content via Twitter. Assuming an equal number of referrals per tweet, I used Google Analytics to project that this link was responsible for over 100 page views. Not too shabby for an extra 20 seconds of work.

OUT-OF-OFFICE REPLY

Another thing you can do is to put your Out-of-Office (OOO) reply to work for you. I see too many people using the generic, "I'm out of the office, with limited access to the Internet, and will be back [date]. If it's urgent, please contact [coworker's name]."

How many e-mails do you get per day? I might get hundreds, so this would be a key time for me to advertise.

Instead of a generic OOO reply, try saying something like this:

> I'm currently traveling, with limited access to the Internet, and will be back [date].

In the meantime, check out our most recent article [company blog post, personal blog post, or recent good press]. If it's urgent, please contact [coworker's name].

This way, you're not wasting those views that you're getting while you're offline. Sigstr will allow your marketing team to create and change signatures across the entire sales team.

Mix in Some Humor

Sometimes adding a little humor into your e-mail can elicit a response. Some people like to go as far as adding funny GIFs or other images to e-mails.

This can work well when a prospect is not responding to you or gives you a negative answer. Once, when I was trying to secure sponsorships for a charity event, I received a "no" from a company that I had thought would definitely say "yes." I knew my audience, so I went for it. I sent over a picture of a really cute dog looking sad. It was exactly what I needed to get the company to give it more serious thought. At the time, I thought it was a reach. Now I'm not afraid to use this approach.

People also like to do this in what is referred to as a "break-up e-mail." Just don't overdo it, and know your audience.

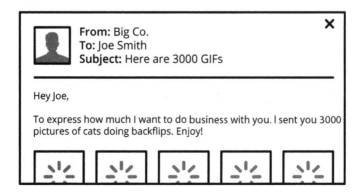

Figure 15.1 Too Many GIFs

According to Craig Rosenberg, proven sales thought leader and author of the Funnelholic blog:

> Embedding GIFs in e-mails can work in certain contexts. It is important to focus on key areas like college, hobbies, puppies, etc. Note: this is best for social media managers, marketing, PR, etc. Don't send GIFs to digital security officers. Know your audience and use this method when appropriate.

Also check out FunnyBizz for injecting humor into all of your sales collateral and operations.

Frenemies

Salespeople are almost always taught to connect with their prospects on LinkedIn. What they aren't taught is how to configure their privacy settings. Therefore, if you are connected to someone and they haven't fixed their settings, you can see when they have a new connection.

Now why am I telling you this? First, connect with sales reps at your competitor's companies. Most of them probably haven't played around with their settings and won't think anything of it when you ask to connect. Once you're connected, keep an eye on whom they connect with. When they connect with a prospect, you'll be notified via a news feed and you can send them a very well-timed e-mail. Just don't mention how you knew to send them an e-mail at the perfect time.

Stay Relevant on Twitter and LinkedIn

When you are involved in a deal at any stage, you always want the customer to be thinking about you. This means that you need to stay on his or her radar. The best way to do this is through LinkedIn and Twitter.

On Twitter, Follow, Favorite, Retweet, Respond. All of these show up on the Twitter notifications tab with your name, image, and handle.

For LinkedIn, try a tool called SearchQuant. It will allow you to select a subset of LinkedIn profiles based on an attribute like vice president (VP) of sales and then it will automatically view VP of sales profiles. In the VP's account, it will show that you viewed his or her profile, thus coming up on the VP's radar.

OTHER UNIQUE SOLUTIONS FOR HACKING SALES

MailLift

Go offline with MailLift, which sends handwritten letters to customers in bulk for you. You might not have physical addresses for your accounts, but you should start collecting them. You need to know what office your target customer is in, and find the corporate address. Once you have that, send the target customer a letter using MailLift. You supply MailLift with a template, as you would in an e-mail campaign, and a list of contacts, and MailLift will write the letters and send them out. You'll have a lot less competition getting in front of someone in his or her physical in-box, and the target customer will appreciate the gesture. Rarely do people send physical letters anymore, so you'll look good.

Also check out Postable for handwritten notes.

As a follow-up to this, I also recommend sending the main decision maker a gift basket after a deal has been closed. This is only for deal sizes of a certain amount, but it will go along well when it comes time to resign or up-sell, and it starts the relationship off on a good note.

After I graduated from college, two friends and I started a business in which we sold real estate agents on running their social media for them. The goal of this business was to make American money while living abroad in Central America, which we did successfully. When we'd close a new account, we'd send the women flowers through 1-800-FLOWERS and the men unique cookies. They would arrive almost instantly. Even though our deal sizes were $600 to $1,500, it was worth it to send $30 worth of fresh flowers or cookies to their offices.

What happened next was fascinating. Other real estate agents from that office would see the flowers or cookies arrive and inquire. They would then call us and order a social media package for themselves.

Sending the flowers was a great way for us to indirectly advertise our services to the rest of the office. People like to feel special. Go the extra mile, even after—especially after—the deal has closed.

Active Admin

Try out Active Admin, a Ruby on Rails plug-in, as a way to track trials and uncover accounts to follow up that are in the database of users. It's almost like a Dashboard-as-a-Service, and it was designed for nontechnical users, so anyone can get the most out of it. You can create a dashboard from Salesforce data or from your own server's back-end data that your sales and customer success teams can easily sort through.

Olark

Olark is a live chat tool that sits on your website and allows you to talk with inbound leads in real time. By using Olark, you can do a lot of the discovery and needs assessment before your leads ever even make a call. You can have marketing development reps (MDRs) or sales development reps (SDRs) arrange to take turns managing the chat and qualifying leads.

In addition, you can create a team that is completely outsourced, either in the Philippines or locally (Phoenix, Austin, Omaha) to control the sales inquiries and pass them to your account executives (AEs), once they're ready.

Whoever figures out the on-page chat, lead qualification system that cuts out the in-house MDR and outsources it completely will have a massive advantage. The team can then take that saved budget and put it toward driving more inbound sales. This becomes infinitely scalable, without the need to invest in more capital, and should drive a lot of qualified leads to AEs.

I recommend testing Olark out if you think you have a service and a team that can pull it off. Let me know how it goes!

Also check out Zopim, LiveChat, LivePerson, BoldChat, Help-Flow, and SaleMove.

Twilio

Twilio is an application program interface (API) that allows you to build custom voice and SMS solutions. You can choose to use this in your cadence by leaving customers generic voicemails or text messages.

You can template these things. Here is an example:

Hey, [First Name],
     It's [Name] from [Company]. I sent over an e-mail earlier regarding how we can help you with [product value]. Please [enter ask here] . . .

Sales from the Streets

For more tips and tricks from top sales professionals around the world, check out the free app called "Sales from the Streets," created by John Barrows and friends. It brings the sales community together to share what's working and what isn't when sales reps are closing deals.

The tips are broken down into categories that span every stage of the sales process, along with other critical aspects of sales, like preparation and motivation. Since the video tips are all actionable and less than three minutes each, they can be used immediately for specific sales situations or can be digested during a sales rep's downtime, like while commuting to work or waiting in line for coffee.

You can also record your own videos and share them with others to help build your own personal brand and presence in the profession.

I always like to see salespeople helping salespeople.

Visit www.SalesHacker.com/library for more sales hacks that we couldn't fit into this book.

CHAPTER **16**

The Wrap-Up

In this book, we have discussed the entire sales process from the salesperson's perspective and have showcased over 100 tools for the modern salesperson.

Your takeaways should be:

1. How to figure out your ideal customer profile (ICP)

2. How to map your total addressable market (TAM)

3. How to find the companies in your TAM and harvest accurate data

4. How to build lists of potential buyers

5. How to find the contact information of potential buyers at scale

6. How to find different strategies for targeting prospects

7. How to properly segment lists

8. How to look at the messaging process and how to track, measure, and optimize your outbound e-mails

9. How to implement outsourcing and how to hire, train, and manage virtual assistants

10. How to pick a CRM system that best fits your needs

11. The best ways to nurture and follow up leads

12. The process of preparing for your first call

13. How to negotiate, handle objections, and close the deal

14. How to navigate introductions, how to phrase introductions, and how to get your point across

15. The importance of asking for referrals

16. How to use bonus sales hacks

Now you are ready to put everything to good use.

I'll leave you with this: if you or your team embraces this new era in sales, you will be infinitely more effective than your competitors, and you will leave them in the dust. You will win because distribution is king, and these tools will allow you to *own* distribution at a repeatable and scalable level. Always be testing, measuring, and optimizing, no matter how good the numbers are. You can almost always do better.

Again, this book and list of tools was created and curated for sellers, not managers. This is why we did not dive into software that is geared toward sales team performance, hiring, and management, such as the following:

- Ambition
- Rivarly
- SalesHood
- Guru
- InsightSquared
- Highspot
- Influitive
- Gogohire
- Hired
- ExecVision
- HireVue
- VisiStat
- and many others

If you have ideas, success stories, or feedback, I would like to hear from you. Please be sure to tell me on Twitter @saleshackerconf or tweet to me personally at @maxalts. I'm always on the lookout for companies and individuals who are doing interesting things in sales.

Visit us at www.SalesHacker.com/library for more resources and bonus material on sales hacking.

RESOURCES AND PROGRAMS

SALES HACKER PROGRAMS

- Check out our content engine for top sales leaders and up-and-coming entrepreneurs at www.SalesHacker.com.

- Get involved in a local Sales Hacker Series meetup near you. We're in 30 cities around the world and are looking to expand to as many cities as possible.

- Attend an upcoming Sales Hacker Conference to recruit, connect, and learn from the best sales reps.

- Check out our Sales Hacker Job Board for the best jobs in sales.

- Join the action in our Sales Hacker Community LinkedIn Group, and start or engage in discussions with top sales leaders.

- Stay tuned for our upcoming Sales Hacker Veterans Training Program, in which we train war veterans to become sales development reps (SDRs).

- Check out Sales Hacker Consulting for sales teams of all sizes and stages; it is looking to build well-oiled sales machines.

- Visit us at www.SalesHacker.com/library for more resources and bonus material on sales hacking.

SUGGESTED READING FOR SALES HACKERS

Publications

- *SaaStr* by Jason Lemkin
- *Bothsidesofthetable* by Mark Suster
- *For Entrepreneurs* by David Skok
- *The Boron Letters* by Gary Halbert

- *The Funnelholic* by Craig Rosenberg
- *A Sales Guy* by Jim Keenan
- *Science of People* by Vanessa Van Edwards
- *JillKonrath.com* by Jill Konrath
- Blogs of the companies listed in this book

Books

- Adamson, Brent, and Matthew Dixon. *The Challenger Sale: Taking Control of the Customer Conversation* (London: Portfolio, 2011).

- Bertuzzi, Trish. *The Sales Development Playbook: Build Repeatable Pipeline and Accelerate Growth with Inside Sales* (New Hampshire: Moore-Lake, 2016).

- Greene, Robert. *The 48 Laws of Power* (New York: Penguin Books, 2000).

- Keenan, Jim. *Not Taught: What It Takes to Be Successful in the 21st Century that Nobody's Teaching You* (A Sales Guy, 2015).

- Konrath, Jill. *Agile Selling: Get Up to Speed Quickly in Today's Ever-Changing Sales World* (London: Portfolio, 2014).

- Mandino, Og. *The Greatest Salesman in the World* (New York: Bantam Books, 1968).

- Roberge, Mark. *The Sales Acceleration Formula: Using Data, Technology, and Inbound Selling to Go from $0 to $100 Million* (Hoboken, NJ: John Wiley & Sons, 2015).

- Ross, Aaron, and Jason Lemkin. *From Impossible to Inevitable: How Hyper-Growth Companies Create Predictable Revenue* (Hoboken, NJ: John Wiley & Sons, 2016).

- Ross, Aaron, and Mary Lou Tyler. *Predictable Revenue: Turn Your Business into a Sales Machine with the $100 Million Best Practices of Salesforce.com* (PebbleStorm, 2011).

ACKNOWLEDGMENTS

I would like to give special thanks to the people who helped with this book:

My dad, David Altschuler, who held me accountable for writing this book while I traveled in Bali.

My mom, Karen Altschuler, who probably doesn't understand a word of this book but supports me in whatever I decide to do with my life.

The original Sales Hacker group: Zander Ford, Ryan Buckley, Tawheed Kader, and Matt Ellsworth, who were all, in one way or another, instrumental in helping me launch Sales Hacker.

The guys who frequently came together for the early meet-ups: Zack Sinclair, J. Scott Zimmerman, Ilya Lichtenstein, Travis Wallis, Brian Kelly, Justin Mares, David Nihill, Jason Lemkin, and others.

To my contributors: Matt Cameron, Daniel Barber, John Barrows, Craig Rosenberg, Emmanuelle Skala, Aaron Ross, John Marcus, Scott Britton, Kyle Porter, Heather R. Morgan, Jorge Soto, J. Ryan Williams, Steli Efti, Jeff Hoffman, Vanessa Van Edwards, Farlan Dowell, Mark Roberge, Kevin Gaither, Ralph Barsi, Wade Foster, and many more.

To all of the founders and employees of the companies who spoke with me.

To Udemy for taking a chance on me.

To my Sales Hacker team, which keeps the train moving.

And last, but certainly not least, a big thanks to the Sales Hacker supporters during the past few years—speakers, sponsors, attendees, readers, contributors, promoters, volunteers, and back-patters. You all rock, and I hope Sales Hacker will continue to provide value in your lives and careers.

Please follow me @saleshackerconf and join the Sales Hacker Community.

A portion of the proceeds of this book's sales will go toward supporting the San Francisco-based charity, Muttville Senior Dog Rescue.

ABOUT THE AUTHOR

Max Altschuler is the CEO and founder of Sales Hacker, Inc. He's always been fascinated with sales, psychology, technology, and entrepreneurship, and he considers himself an entrepreneur first and a salesman second.

Max was the first sales hire at Udemy, an online education company. He built the process that launched the instructor side of its marketplace. Udemy recently raised a $65 million series D round of funding, with a value in the hundreds of millions of dollars.

Max learned much of his sales hacking while he was onboarding experts and building out supply, with very few resources.

He replicated the Udemy model when he was VP of business development at AttorneyFee, which was later sold to LegalZoom and now operates as LegalZoom Local. He's worked with many SaaS, marketplace, and advertising technology companies along the way and truly loves finding new ways to help salespeople become more efficient.

Max started Sales Hacker, Inc. to help other start-ups with fewer resources sell their products and services to large corporations.

Max has a Bachelor's Degree in Interdisciplinary Studies from Arizona State University. He is originally from Syosset, New York, and currently resides in San Francisco, California, when he's not traveling to help people hack sales. He's visited over 70 countries and is still counting.

If you're interested in having Max speak at your event or contribute to content, contact him at getmax@saleshacker.com.

For other inquiries about Sales Hacker events or opportunities, contact marketing@saleshacker.com.

Follow Max on Twitter at @maxalts.

Connect with Max on LinkedIn at www.linkedin.com/in/maxaltschuler.

INDEX